Love within Limits

'A great love song is a moment of ecstasy frozen into
words . . .' writes Lewis Smedes. Writing in a
perceptive, meditative style, he explores how the
ideal of love can be lived out within the limits of
ordinary life.

What is the difference between self-seeking and
self-giving love? What is at the root of bitterness and
pride, of happiness and fulfilment? How can we reach
out to find the love that God intended for us? How
can we realize the ideals enshrined in the New
Testament, in particular in the great passage in one of
Paul's letters which the author calls 'God's love song'?

The author's style is both lyrical and immensely
practical. He is acutely aware of people's potential.
His book will be valued by all who want to know
more of love; and who, knowing, want to live it out
in their own experience.

Lewis Smedes is Professor of Theology and the
Philosophy of Religion at Fuller Theological Seminary,
Pasadena, California. He is the author of several
books, including *Sex in the Real World* which is also
published as an Aslan Lion paperback.

To Doris

An Aslan Lion Book

M. O'Neill

Love within Limits

The ideal of love in everyday life

Lewis Smedes

LION PUBLISHING

Copyright © 1978 William B. Eerdmans Publishing Co.,
Grand Rapids, USA.

First UK edition 1979.

Lion Publishing,
Icknield Way, Tring, Herts.

ISBN 0 85648 190 4

Printed in Great Britain by J. W. Arrowsmith Ltd., Bristol.

Contents

I will show you a more excellent way.

If I speak in the tongues of men and of angels, but have not love, I am a noisy gong or a clanging cymbal. And if I have prophetic powers, and understand all mysteries and all knowledge, and if I have all faith, so as to remove mountains, but have not love, I am nothing. If I give away all I have, and if I deliver my body to be burned, but have not love, I gain nothing.

Love is longsuffering

and kind;

love is not jealous,

or boastful or arrogant or rude.

Love does not seek its own;

it is not irritable

or resentful;

it does not rejoice in evil, but rejoices with the truth.

Love bears all things,

believes all things,

hopes all things,

endures all things.

Love never ends. . . .

As for prophecies, they will pass away; as for tongues, they will cease; as for knowledge, it will pass away. For our knowledge is imperfect and our prophecy is imperfect; but when the perfect comes, the imperfect will pass away. When I was a child, I spoke like a child, I thought like a child, I reasoned like a child; when I became a man, I gave up childish ways. For now we see in a mirror dimly, but then face to face. Now I know in part; then I shall understand fully, even as I have been fully understood. So faith, hope, love abide, these three; but the greatest of these is love.

Paul's first letter to the Corinthians, chapter 13.

A Love Song Is . . .

A GREAT LOVE SONG is a moment of ecstasy frozen into words, a rhapsody of enthusiasm and passion, a metaphor pointing to a moment when the poet was lifted outside of himself to see reality in its ideal form. It charms us with a memory of the ecstatic moment or allures us with the hint that such a moment might yet be possible. A love song is meant to seduce us from routine into a fantasized ideal of perfect love.

God's love song is in many ways like other great love songs. Its human writer St. Paul was taken outside of himself and his ordinary level of experience and given a vision of ideal love. He saw beyond the normal range of human vision, beyond life's patchwork of routine demands and conflicts, into love's ideal form. He crystallized the qualities of love into simple absolutes that have never — save once — taken solid hold in the network of demands that we recognize as our world. And yet his love song seems somehow meant for our living it. It draws a profile of ideal love, but it is too plain for mystic passion. Love is not jealous, does not get angry quickly, endures very much — these are qualities for ordinary living in ordinary days. This is our challenge: to find ways to bring the heavenly rhapsody down into our own worldly realities.

We are not village saints with little to do but find ways to be nice to needy people. We are salesmen trying to survive for our families' sakes against tough competitors. We are directors of business, who know from experience that "love" is not a byword in the board room. We are union stewards in conflict with an obtuse management. We are husbands and wives trying to survive in a marriage where love has wilted into the boredom of mutual toleration. And we are complicated individuals. We have needs, drives, rights, and goals that do not easily harmonize with self-giving love. Love may be simple. Life is complicated.

The purpose of this book is to explore how ideal love — selfless love — can take root in the crevices of real life. I want to see in a realistic way how the power of love can reshape our lives. I am not working out a "love ethic"; I do not lay down the duties of love. I assume that love is a power, and that it enables us before it obligates us. But ideal love does not work in an ideal world. It works within the limits of our ordinary lives. Ideal love is not a supernatural layer patched onto the fabric of life to abolish or cover up our natural drives and needs. The power of selfless love works only within the tissues of our self-interested lives. My object is to see how it works and what happens when it does.

The lines of St. Paul's love song will be our guide. We shall let each line point us to a phase of reality into which love must fit in order to do its work. We want to seize every promise of love's power. But we must let it work within the limits set by all the other legitimate claims and pressing needs of our humanity. Let us see if we can follow the love of Paul's rhapsody down into our worldly reality and make sense of how it works.

1
Love Suffers Long

LOVE IS AN UNCOMMON power to cope with common suffering. Suffering itself takes no talent. It comes to us, takes us captive, pins us down. We are all its victims. Some of us have to suffer more than others. Some are able to suffer with more grace than others. But it is love that enables us to suffer long.

To suffer long seems like a grim return on love. Love, it would seem, holds a poor hand if longsuffering is one of its best cards. But in a world where suffering is almost a law of life, the power to suffer long may be one of life's most needed gifts.

What *is* suffering? Some synonyms that come to mind at once are "pain," "tribulation," "sorrow," "anger." But what all suffering really comes down to is the experience of anything we want very much not to experience. The key here is the phrase "very much." To qualify as sufferers, we must want to be rid of something with such passion that it hurts. But this opens an almost infinite field of possibilities. One day it may be no more than a long wait at the supermarket checkout counter. Another time it may be an incurable cancer in the stomach. Trivial or terrible, each is a form of suffering. Maybe we can at least begin, then, by agreeing that suffering is *having to endure what we very much want not to endure.*

While some things bring suffering to almost everyone they touch, suffering is not really tied to anything in particular. Children usually suffer when their mother dies; but if she is very old or in pain, her children may be thankful for her death. Most people would suffer to hear a doctor tell them, "It's malignant"; yet some people want to die. Almost everyone wants badly to have pain go away; some pains, however, are so close to pleasure that we want badly to have them. In the high-pitch areas of life like sex, agony and ecstasy are sometimes hard to tell apart. And there is no accounting for some of our odd desires. There is probably a hint of masochism in all of us; we sometimes want to feel a pain which we want to go away. That pain may after all bring to us people who stroke our bruised souls, and it gives us a chance to blow off steam. All the while, we hate the pain we are enjoying. In any case, to qualify as suffering we must want very much not to have to experience it, no matter how mixed up our desires are.

We must also notice that to suffer is to be a victim. No matter what it is that we do not want to experience, our suffering takes us captive and pins us down against our desires. The sufferer is a prisoner, stuck with unwanted misery. Loneliness, failure, rejection, oppression, poverty, pain, death — all of them are shackles that bind us against our desire to be rid of them. Suffering means *having to put with,* and this "having to" makes *long*-suffering a minor miracle.

The paradox of longsuffering is that we must *choose* to suffer long. To suffer is to be a victim; to be longsuffering is in a sense to be free. To earn the description "longsuffering" we have to make a decision for what we do not want, choose to live indefinitely with what we hate. This is the paradox that makes longsuffering a creative art of living.

We must be careful not to relieve the tension with a pious twist that turns a *choice* for suffering into a *desire* for suffering. What we desire we cannot claim to suffer. Neurotic hankering after pain does not count as suffering. When we talk about the power to be longsuffering, we are talking plainly about real suffering for a long time. We are talking about digging in daily, renewing over and over again our decision to accept what we desperately do not want and cannot change, making no bones about not wanting it and yet determining to live with it and rejoice *in* it.

The source of power is divine love.

Longsuffering, therefore, is the power to be a creative victim. Longsuffering is not passive. It is a tough, active, aggressive style of life. It takes power of soul to be longsuffering. God's love song is not in praise of merely hanging on. It is in praise of power, the power of affirming and creating life in the midst of suffering.

The power to do this is agapic love. *Agape* is the love modeled by God in his relations with sinners, the love that drove Jesus to the cross. *Agapic love is the liberating power that moves us toward our neighbor with no demand for rewards.* Do not ask whether *you* are *able* to love without thought of reward. Just understand that God's love is the power to move us in that direction.

Erotic love, on the other hand, has no power for longsuffering. *Eros* is desire. It drives us toward something because we are at a loss without it. Eros reaches out beyond one's lonely self because aloneness hurts. Eros moves us toward someone or something that can fill the void we feel and change what we anxiously want changed. Eros is always the passion to overcome suffering, but eros in turn suffers for other reasons. It can be frustrated, when we do not get exactly and enduringly what we long for. It can be betrayed, when people renege on a promise to fill our need. It can be burned out, when what filled us for a season suddenly leaves us empty. Born from suffering, eros is destined for suffering.

That erotic love does not have power to suffer long is its built-in tragedy. It must suffer, but it has no strength for longsuffering. Eros cannot wait: if it does it is only because other powers within us have intervened to slow its pulse and leash its desire. For eros itself — ardent, demanding, ravenous — waiting is too difficult. Eros wants satisfaction soon, or it will "drive us mad." Natural love, then, is the opposite of longsuffering. This is in fact the strength of eros. It drives us towards satisfaction. But its strength is born of its own need, and so it can give no power to suffer long when its need is unsatisfied.

Agape is born of divine strength; therefore, it has the power to be creatively weak. Because it is not driven by ardent need it has power to wait. It gives power to accept life, to find goodness in living while we are victims of situations we despise. This is the only way to explain two attitudes we observe in Jesus toward his own horrible suffering. In Gethsemane we hear him plead with God to be spared the cross that lay ahead. The reality of his suffering is seen in the fact that he did not want the pain. The next day, as he bears his cross to Calvary, he tells the weeping women who follow him: "Don't cry for me." Here we see his power to affirm himself as the loving Lord and free Savior who chose to suffer, chose to be a victim of suffering. He was not a helpless victim of tragedy; he was a powerful person who chose to be weak. He had the strength to become a victim even while he affirmed his own life as free in obedience to love.

There are limits to longsuffering.

How long will love move us to suffer? Is there no limit? Must people with agapic love forever be doormats? Is love always supine? God's love song tantalizes us with the ancient question: *How long, O Lord?* The answer is unclear. *Very* long, perhaps. Maybe as long as you live. Longer than you think possible.

The song tells us of the *power* to suffer long. If love is the power to suffer long, it follows that we ought to suffer long. But we are not thinking now of a duty; we are thinking of love's power to make us able to suffer long. And we cannot make dates on a calendar to measure out love's power. Thus when we ask "How long?" the answer in general is "very long." Perhaps forever. Maybe just until tomorrow. Possibly only until yesterday.

But suffering long is not the same as suffering endlessly. There come moments when suffering must stop. There are some things that we hate and must reject. There are lines to be drawn. The trick is to know when we have reached the moment to draw the line.

God himself draws that line. In shocking disclosure the Bible shows us the tough side of God. We see God deciding not to be a doormat, not to put up with suffering any longer. People — we do not know who they were — had entrenched themselves in an anti-God position and committed themselves to the death of God. God finally let them go. *"God gave them up. . . .* because they exchanged the truth about God for a lie . . ."* (Romans 1:24, 25). His was the creative and compassionate power that had given them their life; and whatever was still good in their lives was a gift of God. But God had to suffer their contempt while he did them good, and finally he refused to suffer any longer. He withdrew his creative mercies. He let them have what they wanted, the death of God in their lives. How did God know that the moment had come to draw the line? Was there some prescribed cutoff point in an eternal blueprint? Probably not. But God knew that there *was* a time to put an end to his longsuffering. And he recognized it when it came.

The word to anyone touched by love's power is something like this: You can and must suffer long; you need not suffer everything interminably. Perhaps you should call a halt now, but remember that your natural inclination is to cut suffering short. Love is your power to suffer longer than you think you can. But only you can tell when you ought to stop.

This is a tension we accept when we live in love's power. We never know beforehand how much and how long love will enable us to put up with things we hate. We do not get a crisp word of relief: "All right, you've put up with it long enough." Nor do we get an imperious order: "You must suffer longer!" We hear only: "Love suffers long." Before you decide to stop suffering, make sure you have not lost contact with love. For the rest, keep attuned to the Spirit and keep your eyes open to what is really going on in your life.

Consider a wife who loves an alcoholic husband. Though her erotic love for him is almost dead, she loves him with the will to do him good with no return on her investment. This agapic love gives her the power to suffer long the agonies alcoholics bring to people who love them. But does love's power to suffer take away all limits on her *calling* to suffer? As we must see, love not only suffers; it seeks justice. It gives people at least what they have coming to them. One thing an alcoholic has coming to him is truth — not merely words truly spoken, but truth that can be seen and felt. Perhaps this may mean that the loving wife will have to make her husband feel the truth by drawing the line and suffering him no more. She may have to leave him. This is not a failure of love. It is the work of love. But only she can know for sure when that moment has come.

Love suffers some things longer than others. Marriage is a special case because marital longsuffering is done within a covenant. Covenants are broken because people live by eros alone and turn their backs on the power of agape. I do not minimize the sufferings of unfilled eros. It can be close to hell on earth. But agape is the power to suffer the pains of frustrated and rejected and betrayed erotic love — and it is the power to suffer them long. How long? No one can draw the line for others. But agapic love is by definition a power that moves us toward another person with no demand for reward. This may be a rule of thumb: when I turn off suffering for the sake of *my* pleasure, I turn it off too soon.

Agape creates a place where eros can be resurrected. It allows time for the revival of mutual love. Rather than trying to compensate for eros, it uses creative and artful enticements in the hope that erotic love will live again. Agape resists our impulse to rush to others for erotic satisfaction and discourages us from hasty divorce. With agape we suffer long, but we suffer with hope. And if we are smart, we also learn the wiles we need to awaken erotic love. Agapic love is not for the witless alone. It suffers long, but it knows the devices necessary for shortening the time of suffering.

Longsuffering is not acceptance of evil.

Love is the power to suffer evil for a long time, but it does not drive us to accept the evil we suffer. To suffer evil takes patience and courage. To accept evil is to capitulate to it in order to escape its horror. Longsuffering is a power developed within reality. Accepting evil is a denial of reality.

Martin Luther King asked his people to suffer long on the painful road to justice. He asked them to suffer bricks and bullets, humiliation and intimidation. He asked them to suffer injustice, but he never asked them to accept injustice nor mute their demands for justice *now*. When black people sang "We shall overcome *someday*," they were giving testimony to their longsuffering, but they were not admitting a willingness to accept injustice until that day. They were asked to accept unjust persons in love. They were not asked to accept the injustice inflicted by unjust persons.

So important is this difference between accepting what we suffer and having the power to suffer it long that to miss it is to confuse some of the deepest issues of life. To accept something is to affirm it. To suffer something is to bear with it even while we reject it. Acceptance may be an act of grace that affirms a *person*. It may be an act of wisdom, as we learn to accept something we mistakenly thought not acceptable. But it is self-deception to accept what is intrinsically unacceptable. Longsuffering is the work of love giving us the power to suffer, but not to accept, what is unacceptable.

A man whose work has given him almost all the meaning he has found in life is suddenly forced to retire early. Must he *accept* enforced idleness? A beautiful young woman is forced by cancer to have a mastectomy. Must she *accept* the loss of her breast? A great athlete is forced out of his career by bone cancer. Must he *accept* the loss of athletic prowess?

All of us at some time suffer mini-deaths. When we lose precious things woven into the fabric of our existence we get a small foretaste of final death. Should agape lead us to *accept* our mini-deaths? The answer is clear: we cannot and ought not to accept these evils. Death in all forms is an evil, the last enemy (1 Corinthians 15:27). And God does not ask us to affirm this final foe of life. He gives us the power of love to affirm life *in spite of death*. But never does love lead us to affirm destruction of life.

There is a heresy that would have us praise God for all assaults on our private lives. That may sound pious, and it may be sincere. But it is false and offensive to God to praise him for evil. The fundamental rule for relating God and evil is this: God is not the cause of evil. "God is light and in him is *no darkness* at all" (1 John 1:15). He wants no credit, certainly no praise, for evil. This is a sensitive nerve of faith, and I wish to say it as plainly as I can: God accepts praise from us *in the midst of evil*. He will have no praise *for* evil.

This means that we must not accept evil's assaults on our life. We must not torture our souls until they affirm what we suffer. Love empowers us to suffer evil, but not to affirm it as a good. That would be an escapist delusion. We must look evil full in the face, see it for the unacceptable horror it is, dare to call it evil — also when it happens to us. For when nature assaults *my* life, it is no less an evil than when it assaults the life of a friend or loved one. A cancer in my own body is an evil just as it would be were it in my child's body. We must be as honest about evil when it attacks us as we are when it attacks others. It is *unacceptable*, plainly and completely. God does not want us to affirm the work of his enemy.

Suffering long has a positive purpose.

When we have the patience to accept ourselves, to accept our future in life, in the face of deep loss or persistent frustration, we are living in love's power. When we have learned to believe that our lives have meaning, when we have opened our hearts to some feelings of joy, when we have seen some rays of light that make us glad, we are longsuffering.

Then courage is added to patience. Courage is the power to resist assaults on our lives — both negatively and positively. In a negative sense courage is the power to be angry at —

indeed, to hate — the evil which assaults us. The person with cancer needs courage to hate the disease that is sapping away his life. The person struck by loss of sight needs courage to hate blindness. The woman who has had a mastectomy needs courage to hate the operation. They must not only be angry, they must not only hate, but they must push that anger and hatred to the surface of their lives and shout to the world: "I hate my cancer."

But then, positively, love comes in, at this moment, as the power to suffer long what we desperately want to go away. Love is the courage to love life and be glad for it. Love is the courage to discover that life is not completely tied to the precious goods we have lost or have not yet found. God's love song does not hammer at us with a demand to be more courageous. This would only defeat us. It says that, with God, there *is* the power. Its name is love.

The model of longsuffering love is God himself. Why, a reasonable angel might ask, did the Creator not give up millennia ago on these stupid rebels? Why does God not call a halt to the frustrations of human history? Why does he not let us finish ourselves off with the doomsday bomb? Why does he not come quickly himself to turn the world into his perfect kingdom? Why does he wait so long before taking decisive action? The answer: God is love. Love suffers long.

God's love is his Yes to a lost world. It is a redemptive Yes, not merely an indifferent or indulgent one. It is a Yes burning with desire for our salvation. An apostle once wrote a letter to some Christians tempted to read God's longsuffering as divine indifference. Skeptics were arguing that love's longsuffering looked more like forgetfulness than patience. "Why does he wait? History just keeps blundering along as it always has. The pain, the violence, the inhumanity — nothing really changes. Surely, his promise is phony." The writer gives the real reason for God's delay: "God is not willing that any should perish, but that all should come to repentance" (2 Peter 3:9). Agape always creates room for reconciliation by suffering long even with what it hates.

So it is with the love that suffers indefinitely. It never

suffers merely for the sake of suffering. Love is not masochistic. It never puts up with things because it does not care much. Love is not indulgent. It does not suffer long because it is afraid to confront wrong and fight it. Love is not cowardly. Love suffers long so that time can be created for redemptive powers to do their work, so that justice can be fought for without hasty and needless violence, so that healing and reconciliation may be possible. Love suffers long so that the evil suffered can be done *away*. Love suffers long so that suffering can finally cease.

And when love gives us the power to suffer long, love also gives us the power to see reasons for rejoicing while we suffer.

2
Love Is Kind

LOVE IS A POWER that moves us to be kind. What are we to understand by kindness? Kindness is the will to save; it is God's awesome power channeled into gentle healing. Kindness is love acting on persons. Such kindness may be soft; it is not weak; tender, but not feeble; sensitive, but not fragile.

Kindness is power.

Our world cannot understand that love is power and that kindness is the work of that power. The German philosopher Nietzsche hated Christianity for encouraging kindness. He accused Christian love of draining strong people by making them kind, driving them to waste their energies on lepers, cripples, and oppressed people. Thus, love weakened the strong of the human race by turning them toward kindness. Were we to rid the world of faith in the Christ, and thus of love, he prophesied, we might again produce supermen. The strong could get stronger and the weak die out.

How wrong Nietzsche was! And how wrong are people today who think along such lines. Far from being weakness, kindness is enormous strength — more than most of us have, except now and then. Kindness is the power that moves us to support and heal someone who offers nothing in return.

Kindness is the power to move a self-centered ego toward the weak, the ugly, the hurt, and to move that ego to invest itself in personal care with no expectation of reward.

It does not take much power to write a small check for charity. It takes great power to enter a leper colony and care, daily and hourly and moment by moment, for scores of lepers whose disease has made them surly and ungrateful. It does not take great power to be a philanthropist, giving to the poor by skimming financial froth into his keenly calculated tax-deductible charities. It takes great power to be a Mother Teresa wrapping tender arms around the wretched poor and bleeding sick in the streets of Calcutta.

To focus on kindness as a form of power, let us consider a few realities about power. We are speaking now of *personal* power, the energy within us to affect persons outside us. Power itself is neutral. It can be harmful and destructive, or creative and helpful. God's power is always the energizer of help, for God is love. But *our* power is always mixed; we use it both helpfully and destructively.

Power is *exploitative* when it is used to diminish the power of other persons. Slaveholders had exploitative power; they were able to push children of God down to the level of horses and shovels, mere tools. When some slaveholders were personally kind to a slave, they were combining healing power with person-destroying power. It was a hideous mixture in which a personal gesture of love's sentiment camouflaged an institutional use of exploitative power. But slavery is only a grotesquely vivid example. Exploitative power is at work whenever we maneuver other people to do what we wish them to do in a way that cheats them of a genuine choice. Exploitative power is inevitably unkind; it is the antithesis of the power of love.

Servant power is personal power used to increase the power of a weaker person. The best example is the power of a parent to nurture a child into an independent personality. Children need a model of personal power. They have to be confronted with the exercise of it. From a parent who demonstrates such power they can absorb psychic and spiritual strength. What sort of power am I referring to? The power to decide, to will consistently, to stick with promises, to demonstrate affection in the midst of tension. The power that gives one the freedom to bow before the Lord and accept his love. The parent who shows these signs of power is demonstrating servant power, which enhances, not diminishes, power in the children.

Servant power is kindness power. To the degree that we have it we are free from anxiety about our own weakness, free to be gentle, tender, openly caring.

There is another kind of power that we may call *collegial* power. This is the power we experience *along with* another person. For instance, both a teacher's power and a student's power grow through mutual criticism. A student's growing power is increased by his courage to criticize a teacher, but it is also increased as he accepts the teacher's criticism. A teacher's creative power, on the other hand, is increased when he integrates his students' criticism of him into his own work. The growth of power is experienced in the same way among a group of scientists. Several centers of intellectual power focus on a single scientific problem. The individual scientists are provoked, challenged, criticized, and, in the end, integrate into their work the work of others. The same collegial power can develop in a more intensely personal way between a wife and a husband.

In Christian communities, collegial power works ideally in mutual ministry to each other's strengths. People minister to each other out of the power that each has been given to discern and rejoice in the potential strengths of others. Too often, collegial power within Christian communities is replaced by negative criticism; the temptation is strong to serve each other *only* by ministering to other people's weaknesses. Collegial power is increased when we minister to one another's strengths, encouraging what is strong to grow still stronger. Collegial power is edifying power, the power to build, to nurture, to add to the strengths of persons.

Within the church collegial power is possible through the shared Spirit. All of us have at least the beginning of power because we are in touch with the power of God, even if we have not grown into it. And the use of this power is collegial: several centers of power encounter each other in love with the result that the power of each person is increased by the power of the others. Collegial power — bracing, challenging, and critical — is compatible with kindness.

Our point in discussing power has been to stress that kindness is not weakness, but a very definite kind of power. Some kinds of power — like exploitative power — are inherently unkind. Other kinds — like collegial power — are consistent with kindness. But kindness itself is a direct expression of servant power. Exploitative power depends on the weakness of other people. We enhance our power, destructively, by discovering, probing, and then exploiting other people's weakness. All of us use this diabolic tactic in some form, whether blatantly or in disguise. Weak people, for example, may use their weakness to exploit the sentimentality of others, and thus turn their disability into exploitative power. Collegial power depends on the strengths of other people. We enhance our power, collegially, by integrating other people's power into our life. In both cases, personal power builds on other people's strengths or other people's weaknesses. Kindness, in contrast, comes directly from the power of love.

Kindness dares to be weak.

The ultimate model of powerful kindness is God. He has no need to exploit the weak to increase his power. He does not have to be stimulated to greater power by the competitive energies of colleagues or the combatant forces of evil. God is self-generating power.

For this reason, he has the power to be indiscriminate in kindness. Since he is not kind in order to get a return on his benevolence, he can be kind to the ungrateful and the selfish (Luke 6:35). The Bible stresses his impartiality: "he makes his sun rise on the evil and on the good, and sends rain on the just and on the unjust" (Matthew 5:45). God's benevolence is uncalculating because it derives from his own power of love. Neither payment for human virtue, nor enticement for human applause, it is the self-generative power of selfless, giving love.

Kindness is love's readiness to enhance the life of another person. But it is more: it is the power to move *close* to another person in order to heal. The pity that wells up in us after watching a television documentary about starving children is not kindness. Kindness is the strength to take the starving child in your arms and feed it at your own breast. Kindness is the power to heal a leper by washing his wounds with your own hands. Kindness is the power to bear another's burdens by feeling his pain in your own soul.

It takes power to be kind because kindness is risky. Unlike God, we often fail to be kind because we dare not risk the consequences. The driving power of love may move us toward kindness, but stop us short when we consider what might happen to us. First, to move toward another person in kindness is to risk misunderstanding. If you are kind to a person of another sex, your action may be seen as a veiled seduction. If you are kind to a person of another race, you may be suspected of being patronizing or subservient. If you are kind to a stranger, you may be rebuffed. Second, after you show kindness to a person, he may take advantage of you. He may become a parasite, getting a grip on your tender impulses and systematically exploiting them. Third, you may, in your amateurish kindness, do things so awkwardly that you end up making a fool of yourself. No one likes to look stupid, perhaps least of all when doing an act of kindness.

The risks in kindness are terrifying. It is far easier to let professional agencies meet welfare needs. They know what has to be done and how to do it. They can cope with cheaters and leeches. But make no mistake about it: if we leave the works of kindness to professionals, kindness will be replaced by efficiency. Love will be lost and welfare will take its place.

This happens if the power of kindness atrophies for fear of the personal risks of kindness.

Kindness is a power born of love. Love is the power of God exercised in apparent weakness. The only way to keep kindness alive in a world where obvious power is prized most is to come back to the cross of Christ, where divine power healed the world by becoming weak within the world. At that focal moment of human history utter weakness was utter redemptive power. The kindness of Christ's cross looks like weakness because it is tender, vulnerable, asks nothing, gives everything, stoops personally to those who are weakest and poorest and ugliest. But it is divine power.

Love moved God to become a person like us. Love led him, as a man, to use his power wholly as servant-power. In love's power he gave himself in kindness. He washed dirty feet, wept with grief-wracked people, empathized with a harlot, entered the lives of the disowned and disdained. All his life he was *powerful* in kindness. But they hanged him; they pounded a rail into the ground, put a crossbar on it, and hanged him till he died. God who is love was hanged to die. The center of power for all the world was weakest of all men.

In this *ultimate* weakness, infinite power was set loose in the world. This is the final truth about power and kindness: ultimate kindness is ultimate power. "The weakness of God is stronger than men," said St. Paul (1 Corinthians 1:25). This is not a riddle about divine weakness. It means that it takes great power to be free enough to be radically kind, to become weak with the weak in order to heal them.

Hence, when in Paul's love song we find the simple line — "Love is kind" — we discover one of the most revolutionary truths in the universe.

Kindness is intelligent and tough.

Love's kindness works within the limits of life's hard realities. For that reason, we must now ask some practical questions about love's limits.

First, does love never count the cost? Is love a reckless kindness? We have limited resources. The love of God does not turn us into super-people. Nor does kindness work in a vacuum. It is exercised within a constant contest between competitors for our concern. For every minute devoted to a neighbor there is one fewer for wives and children. For every dollar given to Charity A there is one fewer for Charity B. For every leper attended to there is one other suffering person who cannot be attended to. Might thoughtless kindness to some people result in unfairness to others? Might a kind person, by mismanaging his resources, actually be unkind?

Kindness must be used with wisdom within a structure of justice and fairness. Consider the role of a teacher. Love moves and empowers a teacher to be kind toward *all* the students; otherwise it will be mere favoritism toward some. Kindness moves the teacher to encourage the dull and the average as well as the bright students. But if kindness forgets about honesty, it will turn into cruelty. For instance, a teacher criticizes a student essay honestly, toughly, pointedly. Not to do this is to rob the student of a chance to grow through an interchange of power. But there must also be a gentleness, a feeling for the student's anxiety about his own abilities. And so kindness *searches* for something in the essay that can be praised, at least for its potential. Kindness compels the teacher to look until finding something worth commendation.

Encouraged, the student may approach the teacher for further help. Love will enable the teacher to give it to him. But this must happen within limits. For there are other students, bright and dull, who have a just claim on the teacher's energy. All of them have a right to a well-prepared lecture the next day. Thus, kindness to the one student is limited by the fair claims of many others.

That we have to measure out the works of kindness in specific instances does not mean that we are withholding kindness. The polite cliché, "Oh, you are *too* kind," is non-sense. Kindness may be stupidly or unfairly directed, but we are never overly kind. It is just that we are limited to practicing kindness within a network of life's demands. Because kindness moves within the limits of fairness, we may have to dispense it carefully, but only in order to prevent foolish kindness from becoming cruel.

If we struggle to be kind within these limits, it will not be unkind to say No to a call for help at times. Kindness without wisdom and honesty easily becomes mere pity, bound to hurt more people than it helps. In *The Heart of the Matter* Graham Greene tells the story of Scoby, who has an affair with a very plain woman. Too "kind" to leave his wife or tell her about the affair, he is also too "kind" to leave the mistress. Such "kindness" reflects not love but pity. Scoby could not distinguish between them, but his dishonest kindness proved poisonous; and it finally killed him. Suicide was Scoby's escape from the pity that tried to pass for love.

Our second practical question is whether all acts of kindness are works of love. Love is always kind, but kind acts are not always loving acts. Some acts typical of kindness are acts of anger, arrogance, or ambition. Those Pharisees who gave their tithes with a great public display were actually using symbols of benevolence to get power over religious people. The rich politician may stand with the poor in order to get their vote. The religious matron sponsoring "charities" for poor children may be saving herself from boredom and reassuring herself that she is splendid in comparison with the poor. The employer who gives a bonus to poorly paid employees may only be trying to manipulate them into accepting unfair working conditions. The husband busy with domestic chores may only want to remind his wife that she is not doing her share. Acts of kindness driven by such demonic energy are not kindness at all.

We do few things from hearts of pure, unalloyed kindness. But this does not take the edge off the power of kindness. It only tells us that we seldom act with clear-cut single motives. If God used only people with utterly pure motives, he would have to wait until his kingdom came to use anyone. Paul does not sing of our being possessed wholly and only by the power of kindness. He does not say that everyone touched by the power will become instantly, totally, and predictably kind. He only says that love is the power that moves us in the direction of kindness. As we *are* moved by love, we will also be moved to be kind.

One more practical question needs asking. Kindness is always a move toward healing. Is toughness out of tune with kindness? Is kindness always gentle? The answer is that kindness sometimes needs to be very hard in order to heal. Kindness may mean forcing an addict to go through the hell of withdrawal. Kindness may mean saying No to a spoiled child. Kindness may mean reporting a crime committed by a friend. Kindness means to withhold what harms as well as give what heals.

When does love require gentleness? When does it require toughness? There are no rules that tell us how to use the power of love in every case. We must calculate the means most likely to achieve the most healing end. Love enables us to use the most useful means; and if healing requires toughness, kindness must be tough.

In touch with God, then, we will be kind. We ought not to be stupidly kind, for love in a competitive world needs both justice and wisdom. Justice must be the framework, and wisdom must give the insight to tell when kindness is just. We will be kind only in part, only imperfectly, for we are not ready for perfection. But influenced by God's love we will have the power to be kind. We will feel the stirrings of a love powerful enough to make us willing to be weak. And we will discover that being able to get close to another person in order to heal is our greatest strength.

3

Love Is Not Jealous

THE CLAIM THAT LOVE is not jealous looks plainly wrong. For jealousy seems to be the constant companion of love. It is conceived in love and nourished by love. If love dies, jealousy dies with it. A love that is not jealous must be a very special sort of love.

Jealousy is a kind of fear — the fear of losing someone. It is also a kind of pain — the pain of being left out of the loved one's life. Jealousy is a feeling of pain at losing touch with someone we love because he or she has been stolen away by someone else.

Lovers are jealous.

Lovers are jealous because erotic love is born of need. Eros is the power that drives me to someone who promises to let me be a partner in every part of life. In love, I need to be the only partner. A man may want the woman he loves to give her whole self to him alone, to invest everything she is in *his* life. When he fears that someone or something is taking part of her life away from him, he feels the pain of loss. When he fears that she is taking a third person into her life, he feels the pain of being crowded out. That pain is jealousy.

Erotic love demands total possession, exclusive rights to another person. Love drives us to want always to be included in the other person's agenda. This is the power of eros, which moves us toward complete fulfilment *in* another person. But such total and exclusive union between two individuals is humanly impossible. Individuals need separation and independence from lovers as much as they need union with them. Therefore, eros is always accompanied by some jealousy, and if a person wants the joys of love, he must be ready for the pain of jealousy.

Jealousy is felt in all forms of erotic love, not only romantic love. Jealousy can happen in a friendship: if a third person becomes a friend of my friend, but not with me, I fear that my friend will be partly stolen from me and I will be shut out from that part of his life which he shares with the third person. That fear is jealousy.

A small boy wakes up one morning to find his mother gone. His father springs the disturbing news that she has gone to the hospital. A few days later she comes home cuddling an undesirable alien — a baby sister. The mother constantly cares for the baby; she even lets it suck her breasts, an intimacy forbidden the older child. The boy fears that he is excluded from his mother's love. That ugly baby has stolen her. The pain is all the worse because everyone says that "we love the beautiful baby." Later that pain of jealousy will return as both children want and feel they need the total love of the mother.

Yes, love is jealous. Yet Paul says that love is *not* jealous. Agapic love is not jealous. The love of this song is not a seeking, grasping, holding love, but a giving love, a love that lets go. It is not the love of need, but the love of power. It is the power to move us toward another person with no expectation of reward — not even the reward of exclusive loving. This is why agape is not jealous.

Jealousy hurts.

Jealousy is not the same as envy. When we wish that we had something that belongs to someone else, we envy. A man may envy a Rockefeller his money. A woman may envy a

Princess Grace her beauty. But this is not jealousy; it brings no sharp, ugly stab of pain. The people we envy are not a threat to us; they only happen to have what we would like to have.

Jealousy is aimed at someone who threatens us, threatens to take away someone we love. The person does not have to threaten to steal our loved one completely. The secretary may take only a slice of professional life away from a wife. A man who shares a woman's love of Mozart may take only a small musical slice of a wife's life from her tone-deaf husband. But erotic love wants all, and to miss one dimension of a loved one's life is to sense a threat to the rest. So jealousy easily turns to resentment, anger, even hatred.

The third person makes you feel left out. You may never have been able to enter your husband's professional life or your wife's love of music, but you did not feel left out of it until someone else shared these parts of his or her life. This third person threatens you with further loss. If she can share his professional life, what will keep her from seducing him into giving more? If he shares a symphony with your wife today, he may share more tomorrow.

People are not the only thieves of persons we need. Impersonal things can also seduce our lovers, stabbing us with jealousy's needle, sometimes even more sharply than losing out to another person. Somerset Maugham relates the fury of Paul Gauguin's wife when he left her in her respectable boredom in London as he took up painting in Paris. Another woman she could have fought. Even without winning, she could have been quite certain her husband would finally come home again. But to lose a lover to oils and vivid shapes and color — this was to lose him forever, and the pain was white hot. For others it may be the stupor of Sunday afternoon football or the fervor of night after night in the study. Whatever it is, when it threatens to take away a loved one whom we want to keep neatly in place on our life's agenda we feel pain — and the name of the pain is jealousy.

No doubt men in general are just beginning to find out what jealousy feels like when its object is something more difficult to confront than a predatory male rival. Women know too — better now than they used to — that erotic love requires movement, a drawing together and a drawing apart, times of union and times of separation, if it is to be kept alive. But today's husbands still have little experience at accepting the fact of the wife's also moving away and returning instead of her standing still while her husband goes away and then returns.

With the woman moving into her own private places and her own private times, life together is never as regular and predictable as it was when the man determined it all. The husband in these circumstances may think that he is only *irritated* because the house is not always as neat as it once was and dinner is not always served at the hour most convenient for him. But this is more than just irritation: the deepest pain is jealousy, the fear that the loved one is being taken away, that she is not possessed whole any more, that she is no longer entirely his own. All this can happen when the enemy that steals her away is nothing more dangerous than a new job at the local library.

Jealousy and envy are different feelings. A student feels no jealousy of the teacher's knowledge; a student feels jealousy when a roommate consistently gets A's while he manages only B's. A merely competent violinist has no jealousy of a Yehudi Menuhin. She feels jealousy when another competent violinist is moved to a higher position in the orchestra than she. We envy without pain. Jealousy is the pain we feel when our role, our position, is threatened by someone close to us. Envy can stimulate us to try harder. Jealousy stimulates us only to resentment of the person who does better.

God is jealous.

Jealousy, however, is not in itself a sin. The love song is not condemning jealousy. God himself is a model of jealousy. "I the Lord thy God am a jealous God," he said from Mt. Sinai. He is jealous for himself. He feels pain when he shares his people with idols.

False gods are fabricated illusions, puny finite objects of ultimate devotion. The idol exists, but the god it pretends to be does not. It cannot exact unconditional allegiance because it does not have the power to support us — or even to condemn us, for that matter. God alone is God, and he knows it. He wants to be what he is, the only God of all creation. He has no intention of playing games with nonentities. He will not compete for worship with the fantasies people project into the role of deity, nor share those whom he loves with a hoax, a nothing, an illusion. But he will share his people with other people.

"Love the Lord your God with all your heart, all your soul, all your mind." The great command sounds much like any romantic love song: "Love me with all your heart. . . ." The difference is that God feels no pain when we share our love for him with a fellow human.

God is not jealous when men and women give themselves to each other. A loving God has filled the world with a profusion of loves. He created us to give ourselves, heart and body, to others besides himself; and he is glad when that happens. God weeps when people think they can love *only* him. He is the first to admit that he alone is not enough for a man or woman. People need people as surely as they need God. Because God knows this, his redemptive love creates a company of love-sharers. People learn how to share each other because they share God's love.

God can share us with other people because of the power that is his love, which moves him to let others be themselves. Consider the work of creation. God wanted the world to be, to be different from him, to be beautiful and powerful in its own way. He did not need to create a photocopy of himself to look at and enjoy, as Narcissus enjoyed himself in the reflection of a pool. He willed other sorts of personal beings to exist in their own way. He allowed them to *be*, really to be themselves, like God and yet very different from him. God does not monopolize existence.

Agape transcends jealousy without destroying it.

Love is the inner power to be happy when someone else shares your friend. Love is the power to rejoice in the superior talent, success, or power of someone close to you. Indeed, love is the power to be glad when another person shares a part of your loved one's life that you cannot share.

Love as the power to share persons originates in a God who could give his Son to win many sons and daughters who would love each other as well as him. Such love knows that sharing a friend is not losing one but only making the circle a little larger. It knows that another person's excellence does not diminish my own or your own, but only adds to the luster of all.

To be loved with this love and to share its power is to overcome fear — even the fear of loss, even the fear of being left out. In other words, this love enables us to transcend jealousy. It overcomes fear as it overcomes self-pity and the insecurity and suspicion of erotic love. So, this love is the power of sharing without being threatened.

But we must not suppose that we can live by agapic love alone. God knows that we must live by erotic love as well. He knows that we are lackluster and empty without eros in our lives. We must follow the longings of our soul for something or someone beyond ourselves to satisfy this need. Because jealousy is the steady companion of eros, however, we will be jealous in this finite, sinful life as long as we love erotically. Where agape enables us, we will rise above jealousy, but we will not eliminate it.

As long as we love with both eros and agape, natural love and Christian love, we will live in creative tension with jealousy. Eros says, "You have a right to be jealous." Agape says, "You can transcend your natural jealousy."

From this tension creative compromises can come. Within marriage eros demands exclusive sexual love; this demand rises from the heart of marriage. Every spouse has the right to jealousy when the heart of marriage is being threatened, nor will agape deny or transcend this right. Agape respects boundaries and limits in life. But where the partnership is not in fact threatened, Christian love is the power to share a husband or wife with another.

Jealousy stabs the deepest when we feel weak, unloved, and righteous. Then it may arouse mean reactions. We are tempted to react to our pain in self-righteous pride, as the "good and noble" spouse being left out in the cold in spite of all our sacrifices. It is when we feel hurt and righteous that we become cruel. Since we are *so* virtuous and the spouse is *so* thoughtless, we feel we have a right to find ways to hurt back.

Jealousy becomes the more cruel the more intense are the expectations of eros and the threats to its fulfilment. If we have nothing else in the world to live for but our lover, we are vulnerable to the worst fits of jealousy. The person who tells someone else, "I *can't* live without you," is threatened at his deepest selfhood when the one with whom he cannot live without has to be shared in the *smallest* way. Such a person always suspects the worst, and this very suspicion prods him to cruel reactions.

Agapic love is the power to diminish the pain of jealousy because it keeps us from expecting too much from another finite person. Agape does not let us give our souls to idols, not even to the idol of the ideal husband or wife or friend. Agape keeps eros from expecting everything in this life. So agape will not let us be so deeply threatened that our very existence seems at stake.

Christian love further diminishes the pain of jealousy because it is the power to share even a loved one, to be thankful that someone else can discover the very qualities in a friend or spouse that you so much appreciate. It is the power, too, to admit cheerfully that you cannot meet all the needs of your loved one or friend and are pleased that someone else can add what you lack.

This love is not jealous. But, remember, agape does not forbid jealousy any more than it kills erotic love. It is the power by which a person can transcend without eliminating the pain of jealousy. In transcending jealousy love can control it, limit it, steer it. Agape will let jealousy do its work, always painful but sometimes stimulating, good work. Let jealousy be a tinge of hurt that reminds us how much we still love and care. Let jealousy be an exciting revelation to the other person that he or she is loved enough to cause pain. Let jealousy be a warning system that protects a marriage by reminding us that we love within limits. But where there is Christian love, the power of agapic giving and sharing will prevent jealousy from building barbed-wire fences of self-protection against any sharing of love and loved ones.

Agape itself is not jealous. Of course not, for agapic love gives others the freedom to search for and grow toward their potential selves and to share themselves beyond the bilateral relationships they have with you and me. Agape is the power of sharing. Hence it is true: love is not jealous.

4
Love Has Poise

LOVE IS NOT BOASTFUL, arrogant, or rude. It is the opposite of these. For love has *poise*.

Boasting is a way of trying to look good when we suspect we are not good. Arrogance is an anxious grasp for power when we fear that we are weak. Rudeness is putting people down in order to try to hold ourselves up. All three result from a loss of balance that comes when we are empty at the center. Love is the power of poise because it provides ballast at the center of our lives.

This, in short, is what Paul means by saying that love is not boastful or arrogant or rude. But we should pull all these things apart in order to get a better look at the forces within them and to see how they fit together.

We boast because we lack poise.

Boasting is our private advertising business, our little campaign to publicize an *image* of ourselves. Sometimes we boast because we suspect that people will not care enough to notice us or be shrewd enough to recognize our assets. Other times we boast out of a fear that our assets are not worth their caring. Anyway, we don't trust things to take their course, to make the proverbial better mousetrap and wait for the world to beat a path to our door. We have to create our image and put it up front in our ego's display case. This is boasting.

Not that there is anything wrong in wanting to be noticed, wanting people to applaud you or buy your mousetrap. But there is something wrong about boasting, and that is that it *always* distorts reality. We boast when we are afraid that, if people do notice us, they will not admire what they see. No one who knows the tricks of impressing people will be a swaggering, blustery braggart. Effective boasting is done through clever use of the right symbols. We use symbols to cover lack of substance, or what we only fear is lack of substance.

Symbols are supposed to point beyond themselves to a greater reality. Think of a wedding ring and what it points to. So we display our symbols to point to our quality of character or our level of success. The symbols we use to boast may be things, like clothes or cars or boats; or people, the friends we cultivate, the names we drop, the people we want to be seen with; or actions, like the parties we go to, or the clubs we join, or the offices we try to win. All these symbols are supposed to point to some good quality of our persons.

Again, there is nothing wrong with us for enjoying praise. Even God enjoys letting us in on his glory so that he can enjoy us while we enjoy praising him. But when we boast, out of fear that we are not worthy of applause, that what we are and do are not good enough to win applause, we demonstrate our lack of poise. We think we need others to keep us on our feet because we don't have enough reality in the center of our lives to keep our balance. To get their reassurance, their support, their respect, we create an image out of our symbols.

We are arrogant because we lack poise.

For the same reason, we are tempted to be arrogant. Arrogance is grasping for *power* that we fear we don't deserve. It is more serious than boasting, which is only a grab for praise, covering for what we suspect is empty inside. Arrogance, by contrast, is a grasp for power we do not have authority to take.

Arrogance is the mark of a person who arrogates. To arrogate means to grasp for power that is not authentic to us. Authenticity gives power. If we have authentic knowledge, we have intellectual power. If we have authentic character, we have moral power. If we have authentic skills of leadership and a mandate to lead, we have power to lead. Such authentically based power is good. But arrogance swipes at power without worrying about authenticity. It is power without authority, arrogated power.

Arrogant people push themselves into leadership in any group. They stride into prominent places while others wait to be invited. They make decisions for groups and assume the others will follow. They set up programs and force others to function within them. Meanwhile, they put on a "leadership" style to convince people that it is very right and natural for people like them to be in charge. Arrogance usually needs to do a lot of boasting to get by.

The arrogant person uses people as stepping stones to power, even the people closest to him. Parents often treat their own children as pawns in their strategy for power — not political power, but psychological and moral power. The arrogant parent wants the child to do well so that he or she can feel good about being a parent and get recognition for the child's achievements. But, in the meantime, the parent manipulates the child to do the sorts of things parents want their children to do. The parent arrogates to himself or herself power over the child, so that the parent can look and feel good. This is arrogance because the authority of parents does not include the right to *manipulate* the child in order to feel powerful. Worse yet, the child is being educated not in love but in manipulation, and is learning that what counts is not what you are, but what you can do to get control of people.

Pride causes arrogance.

The root cause of arrogance is pride, but between the two stands vanity. Pride leaves us vain, and vanity pushes us toward arrogance. The dynamics of this involve three sets of persons. We begin with pride toward God. Pride leaves us with vanity inside ourselves. And vanity pushes us into arrogance toward other people.

Pride is arrogance in a vertical direction. Spiritual pride has to do with how we feel about God. (There are other sorts of pride; but they are very different and perhaps should not even be called pride. If a father is proud of his daughter for winning a tennis match, he is *not* guilty of spiritual pride, but is merely participating with her in the joy of victory.) Pride in the religious sense is an arrogant refusal to let God be God. It is to grab God's status for one's self. In the vivid language of the Bible, pride is puffing yourself up in God's face. Pride is turning down God's invitation to join the dance of life as a creature in his garden and wishing instead to be the Creator, independent, reliant on one's own resources. Never does pride want to *pray* for strength, ask for grace, plead for mercy, or give thanks to God. Pride is the grand illusion, the fantasy of fantasies, the cosmic put-on.

The fantasy that we can make it as little gods leaves us empty at the center. Once we decide we have to make it on our own, we are attacked by the demons of fear and anxiety. We are worried that we cannot keep our balance as long as we carry no more inside our empty heart than what we can put there. We suspect that we lack the power to become what our pride makes us think we are. So we learn to swagger, to bluff, to use symbols to cover up our fears that we lack substance. We force other people to act as buttresses for the shaky ego that pride created by emptying our soul of God. In the words of God's love song, we become arrogant.

Vanity is emptiness. A person who is empty at the center of life is vain, and a vain person is almost always arrogant. Every new situation calls forth the question: "What can I get out of this to support the need of my ego for power and applause?" As he encounters new people, he wonders, "How can this person contribute to my need for applause and power?" He projects his own anxieties onto other people, so when others come to him he wonders, "What is this person's pitch? What does he want from me?" Life becomes a campaign to use people to support oneself and a constant battle to avoid having others use oneself that way. Vanity creates the need to use people because we cannot keep our balance spiritually if we are empty at the center.

Because arrogance is born in personal vanity, arrogant people are driven without mercy. They can never get enough power to fill the soul's needs or enough respect to overcome the fear that they deserve less than they are getting. This is why many people waste their sad lives trying to please people. Some cannot cope, and become depressed, even suicidal, as they despair at ever deserving to be liked. Others are driven to more and greater achievements, always in order to please someone. In all cases, the same emptiness that makes people arrogant makes them miserable. Vanity is a relentless driver.

When vanity creates arrogance, it creates a monster. Power for power's sake is dangerous power, which is why vain people are dangerous when they get power. They want power only because it puts them on top of other people. Thus, other people are either supports for their empty souls or are enemies to be demolished. And power is used, not as the means to move the system toward the service of people, but as the means of keeping one's own balance, of staying on top, without spiritual weight inside.

Since the arrogant person can think of power only in terms of being more powerful than other people, he will always be fearful that somebody else will threaten his power. To cover his insecurity, he becomes even more arrogant, and is ready to use *any* means to make his power more secure. This is why rulers become tyrants, oppressors of people. It is also why ordinary lovers may become manipulators and even sadists.

Arrogance causes rudeness.

We can easily see why God's love song connects rudeness with arrogance. Rudeness should not be confused with crudeness. The crude person is one who has not learned the manners of society. The rude person is the one who is so hell-bent on staying upright that in his anxiety he cuts and bruises anyone who threatens him, even as he uses anyone who can help him.

Rudeness, too, comes from emptiness. The poised person, by contrast, can quietly fit in any time or place without having to call attention to himself. He does not have to *look* strong by bullying the servants or manipulating the powerful. Arrogance drives us to be rude to people who have nothing to offer us, nothing to help us look good, while we use the devious tactics of boasting on those who have something to offer. Vanity, emptiness at the center, leads us to see life as a trade-off. What I can get out of you determines what I will give you. If you have nothing to offer, I can be rude to you.

Love is never rude, because love is the power that moves us toward people for their good alone. Agapic love is never a trade-off.

Agapic love overcomes arrogance and boasting.

Our focus now shifts to the opposite of arrogance and boasting — humility, a willingness to accept the real relationship between God and one's self. It is the strength of accepting one's status as a dependent creature — an invaluable, responsible, creative person, but still a creature who needs the energy of God to exist at all. Moreover, humility is the grace to accept oneself before God as a sinner, to admit spiritual emptiness, and to plead for and accept forgiveness. The flipside of this self-acceptance is that humility is the gift to acknowledge God as Creator and Saviour.

Humility is the catalyst for a realistic view of oneself that dares to affirm both sides of creature life under God. In realism we admit our private emptiness, so that the center of our lives can be filled by the Spirit of Christ. We admit weakness and claim strength at the same time. Realism relieves us of the need to boast and be arrogant because it frees us from having to fill our inner emptiness by other people's praise or our own power. Our emptiness is filled for us by God.

The realist can accept reality in its two-sided need — of power and grace from God — and its two-sided strength — of being God's image and Christ's disciple. By simply accepting reality, she can move on to live with others and for others. The humble realist does not grovel or make herself out to be worthless or shrink before great thoughts and high goals. A humble person is lowly of heart, but may be high-minded.

A person who sets her heart on great things is high-minded. Sensing her own potential, she gracefully moves out toward achievement of good and notable things. Such a person does not fear recognition or despise honor. Indeed, she likes what is truly honor*able*, worthy of honor, and so does not refuse honor out of false modesty.

High-minded people also appreciate power. But they do not want power in order to go one up on other people. They want power because there are many good things one cannot get done without power. The person who says at the age of thirty that he or she intends to become president or prime minister is not necessarily arrogant. He or she may be high-minded, seeking power in order to do good for others. Arrogance and high-mindedness are not the same. Love is not arrogant, but love can be high-minded. This tells us that love has poise, the power to stand up straight. It suggests security and grace and freedom from worries about stumbling and making a fool of yourself.

The word "poise" originally referred to the weight placed in the center of a sailing ship for balance. This ballast set the keel deep enough into the water to keep the ship from capsizing. By ourselves, without God, we are too light at the center; we are like a ship without *poise*, likely to capsize. We boast and become rude and arrogant, in the hope that praise from others and power over others will act as external braces to make up for lack of centered weight. It is God's love that can give us centered weight on the inside.

"Weight," of course, is just a manner of speaking. God does not make us heavy. In fact, God's love makes us light. It gives us poise not by telling us we cannot fall, but by assuring us that if we do he will set us right again. As the love of God keeps coming into us from outside, we can forget about our emptiness and move on toward others. As we realize that our power is not generated by ourselves, inside, he begins to fill us with himself and his love. As long as we love, the promise that gives us poise is sure: "God abides in us and his love is perfected in us" (1 John 4:12).

5
Love Does Not Seek Its Own Rights

LOVE DOES NOT SEEK its own. We shall devote two chapters to this line of God's love song.

Let us first translate this line as: "Love does not seek its own *things*." That is, love does not drive us to get and keep what is properly ours — our *property* — for which we need not thank anyone. If we do not get these things, we are victims of an injustice.

Justice is done when everyone gets what is coming to him or her. We seek justice when we seek "our own." We *have* justice when we get "our own." Now, the song tells us, agapic love does not move us to seek our own. Does this mean that love does not want us to claim our rights? Could it mean that God's love is not on the side of justice for the loving Christian?

Can we be loving and assertive?

Throughout the Bible God's demand for social justice sounds forth in clear and powerful tones. "Justice, and only justice, you shall follow, that you may live and inherit the land which the Lord your God gives you" (Deuteronomy 16:20). This was the command to Israel as they entered the land of promise. Justice was to be the key characteristic in God's country. At the other end of history, the land of promise is the "new earth," the kingdom of God, where God himself will rule. Here justice is not a command, but a promise: "According to his promise we wait for new heavens and a new earth in which justice dwells" (2 Peter 3:13). Between the command at the beginning and the promise at the end, God's prophets continually command and promise justice. "Let justice roll down like waters," thundered Amos (5:24). Meanwhile, the comforting promise was repeated: the Messiah shall come, to bring the kingdom of God, "to establish it, and to uphold it with justice. . ." (Isaiah 9:7). Let it be said, then, that the cry for justice, rising like an agonized anthem from the heart of all people, echoes God's demand and God's promise for mankind.

God commands justice because he invested human beings with rights at creation. Essential to Christian faith is the belief that all persons confront each other with rights as human beings. Every person was made as God's image and thus bears the imprint of God in his or her very being. This is why a person's rights must be respected by other human beings. No one has to carry a card to certify membership in the company of those who have rights or prove that he or she is valuable enough to have rights. It seems unthinkable, then, that God's love would cancel out human rights. For this would be to cancel justice.

Love, as the self-giving power of a just God, *seeks* justice. For love can do no less than see that our neighbor gets what is rightfully his. Love is ready to do more, but it cannot do less. Anyone who says that lovers need not care about justice is talking nonsense. How can we want to meet our neighbor's need unless we want him to have what is his by right?

God's love song, however, tells us that love does not move us to seek justice for *ourselves*. This is the catch. Love will drive us to move heaven and earth to seek justice for others. Love may lead us to take up arms and overthrow tyrants for the sake of justice for tyranny's victims. It may drive us to the Supreme Court for the sake of justice for others. Love may send us into the streets to throw a community into turmoil for the sake of justice for oppressed people. But love does *not* move us a millimeter to seek justice for ourselves. "Love does not seek its own."

Why should love and justice be at odds in this one place — the heart of the loving person? As a loving person you have rights; you are still God's image. God does not deal away your rights in order to give you love. You are still a member of human society. Why, then, does love not exercise those rights and seek justice for itself?

Love does not cancel anyone's rights. But agapic love moves one freely to *forgo one's claim* on what one has a right to have. God's love does this to every person it touches. It comes as a power in life that moves us to pass up our chances to seize what belongs to us.

Of course we do "seek our own," and we seek it with vengeance. No child has to be taught to scream for what is his when someone grabs it away. As we get older, we learn to let the system scream for us. How many of us — out of love — refuse to make a claim on our auto insurance when someone bends a fender? What Christian businessman refuses to send bills to his customers? How many Christian senior citizens send back Social Security checks? Seeking "our own" is built into our system, and for the most part Christians are card-carrying members of the "self-seekers" club.

If, indeed, we find fault with ourselves at all on this score it is for giving up our rights too quickly. We fear that we lack assertiveness, so we take courses in "assertiveness-training." We pay stiff fees to therapists to be cured of the neurosis of "not seeking our own." Most of us want to be secure people who confidently assert our claims to what is coming to us.

The question is, Are our assertions of rights — whether stumbling or confident — condemned by love? Do we truly have love only when we become dumb sheep, ready prey for the wolves of the world? Do the standards of agapic love stamp us as spiritual second-raters whenever we claim what is ours by right?

Think of some concrete examples. Ought a black Christian never to fight to get for himself the opportunities the law, too easily circumvented, grants him? Must a loving woman always put up with less pay than a man receives for the same work? Must a businessman never demand payment for goods delivered? May a worker never strike for better working conditions? The answer seems very clear. Of course, we ought to fight for our rights. To ignore them is to ignore reality. Rights are built into life. To give them up must be a dishonor to our creation as God's image. Justice requires us to seek our rights.

Justice and love have their roots in the same God. They should co-exist as allies. Yet love moves us to deny what justice urges us to demand. How can we bring the two together in creative tension if not harmony?

When may we seek our rights?

Agapic love takes root in our lives along with other powers. It is the "more excellent way," not the only way. As agape pierces to the center of our lives, it enters a network of other powers and other needs. Justice is one of these powers and one of these needs. We cannot love within the realities of this world without coming to terms with our rights as they exist in interlocking relationship with the rights and needs of others.

There is a way to cope with this tension which recognizes the priority of self-denying love and also admits the legitimacy of self-asserting justice. It involves the distinction between *means* and *ends*. We can think of our rights as a means or as an end. When we assert our rights in order to protect or foster a neighbor's rights, they are a means; when we assert them purely to satisfy ourselves, getting our rights becomes an end in itself.

1. Seeking our rights for the sake of others' rights. The key is the rights of the neighbor. If I can help my neighbor get his rights by asserting my own, agapic love is on the side of asserting them. But if sacrificing my rights is required in order to help my neighbor get his rights, agapic love will move me to make the sacrifice. Seeking your own rights is thus consistent with agapic love to the extent that doing so helps a neighbor.

Let us look at a simple example — even though in real life

the situation is always a lot more complicated. Suppose that a man borrows five hundred dollars from me. If he does not pay me back according to our agreement, I will not be able to pay my creditors — who have a right to what I owe them. I will probably give less to help others if I have less; so if I do not press my claim on that five hundred dollars, I may very well keep other people from getting their rights and be discouraged from doing a work of love. And if I do not press my claim, my wealthy debtor may be encouraged to ignore other debts, perhaps to people who need the money more than I but cannot press their claim as rigorously as I can. In some cases, then, agapic love will best be served if I do seek my rights.

A disabled or retired father demands his pension. If he does not press his claim to it, his wife and children will suffer unjustly. An oppressed person will fight for his own freedom. Not to fight is to help doom others to oppression. Ministers of the gospel, too, must insist on the right to a decent salary. If they are to be poor, it ought to be because they freely choose the ministry of poverty, not because a church is withholding what is properly coming to them. What all these cases demonstrate is that we live in a network of claims that we make on others and claims that others make on us. The life of love has to find its "more excellent" way within this real world.

2. Seeking our rights to fulfil our calling. A second occasion for seeking our own rights goes deeply into the very reason we exist. We were created for a purpose, to *do* something with our lives. Everyone is set on earth to follow a vocation, and we must sometimes assert our rights in order to fulfil that calling.

It must be immediately added that love's view of God's purpose must be an unselfish one. The claim to be following a vocation has often been an excuse for shortsighted and hardhearted selfishness. Anyone can claim to have a calling to make a fortune: that is why "work ethic" has such a bad name in our time. But the misuse of the truth in capitalism does not make it an untruth: we *are* born into the world with a job to do. And the job we have to do is the job of taking care of God's world and God's people. All of us are stewards, and agapic love moves us to be good stewards.

Thus, whenever someone gets in the way of my steward-ship, I must somehow remove that obstacle. I must demand my rights so that I can take care of my corner of God's earth. I do not get my rights by doing my duty: I have my rights in order to do my duty. The difference is crucial. I have rights so that I can be a steward of the time and the space God entrusted to me. But God entrusted them to me, not for my sake, but for the sake of my brothers and sisters. This is another reason why agapic love will sometimes endorse fighting for one's rights.

3. *Seeking the right to truth.* There is a third claim for one's own rights that love encourages, the claim of *truth*. We must press our right to the truth about ourselves. We have an undeniable right to be what we truly are and to be known as what we are. What we are is the image of God. I need not prove that my existence has some "redeeming social value" to demonstrate that I am a member in good standing of God's image-bearers. I need merely be, as a person. I may have an IQ of 65. I may be senile, weak, helpless, of marginal use to an efficient society. But I must demand my right to be viewed, respected, and treated as a creature with the dignity and destiny of God's own child and partner.

God himself is our model. He asserts himself by insisting on his own divine holiness. Holiness is God's zeal for the truth about himself. His revelation of holiness is a manifesto of his inalienable right to be known as the exclusive Lord of creation. Holiness is God's "jealousy" of his own reputation. It is not conquered nor whittled down by his love, for to diminish it would be to diminish God, and God will do anything for man except stop being God.

* * *

We have said that love does not always require us to abandon our rights, and we have mentioned three cases in which self-denying love would not require us to sacrifice our rights: (1) when the sacrifice would jeopardize the rights of other people or miss an opportunity to protect their rights; (2) when the sacrifice would prevent our functioning as God's stewards; and (3) when the sacrifice violates the truth of what we are.

It is love itself that justifies seeking our rights in these cases. For love is the power that moves us toward other people without demand for reward. In these instances, seeking our rights is necessary in order to move toward the neighbor in love.

But we must still face up to love's impulse to *sacrifice* our rights. Often, more often than we suppose might be practical, love does move us to give up our rights to what truly belongs to us. No one can predict when such moments of sacrifice will come or decide for someone else when it is time to give up a claim to justice. Each of us has to recognize it for himself or herself.

What are the guidelines for sacrificing rights?

There may, however, be some rules of thumb to help us. The general rule is that living in love we are always ready to forgo our rights for the sake of our neighbor. Love always pushes us to the uttermost limits, but there are limits set to this general rule. These limits are set by reality, not by selfish whim. Let me suggest three guidelines to help us recognize the limits for sacrificing rights.

1. We may not force other people to sacrifice their rights. Let us say that a loan officer in a bank is moved by love to make an interest-free loan to a poor family. If he does so, he will force other people to risk the savings they have invested in the bank. He manipulates them into an "act of love" without their free decision. Hence, his impulse of love, if followed, involves him in injustice to other people. If he is truly moved by love, he must find a way to sacrifice his own resources to help the family.

2. We ought not to sacrifice our rights if doing so would hinder the progress of rights for others. A tired black lady, sitting in a bus one hot afternoon in Montgomery, Alabama, refused to move from the front of the city bus. If she had abandoned her right to human dignity, she might have slowed the drive toward black people's rights in this country. A sixteenth-century monk, harassed by papal powers, refused to sacrifice his right to speak the truth as he had learned to know it. Had he given up that right, he would have postponed the right of countless people to know and speak religious truth. As love did not compel Rosa Parks to the back of the bus or Martin Luther to accommodating recantation, so love does not compel any of us to sacrifice our rights if to do so would cost other people precious rights.

3. *Any sacrifice of our rights must leave us in a state to love effectively another day.* Love is without limit, but lovers are limited. Each of us has a certain supply of energy and only so much time and power to expend it. Even when we love with the power of God's love, we are not God. Because our powers of love are limited, we must use them today with prudence so that we will have resources for love's work tomorrow.

Prudence will sometimes set limits to self-giving for the sake of *effective* love. We may have to husband our resources, demand our tax credits, claim our dividends, in order to love more effectively. We need to claim our right to know the facts about well-publicized charities in order to avoid wasted love. We may need to fight tooth and claw within the adversary system of justice to sustain our rights. All the while, if we are in touch with God, we will be ready to drop our rights and become a doormat, in any situation where love compels it.

Love needs discernment.

Being willing to sacrifice our rights is one thing; knowing *when* is another. Love needs the sensitive gift of *discernment*. No built-in computer calculates for us the right time to fight and the right time to surrender. God did not provide a manual that tells us which way to go when love and justice pull in opposite directions. The secret of knowing lies with the personal power to discern. Discernment is the ability to see the difference between things. It is the power to see what is really happening, to see what is really important and what is not important. Discernment is insight — the power to see *inside* of things. It is the strange and subtle ability to see beneath the surface, to sense the personal factors of any situation, and to grasp what spiritual issues are really at stake. When we are directly involved, discernment is insight into the mixture of motives moving our own hearts. Working its way through real life, love needs the gift of discernment to focus its drive toward others in helping service.

Discernment is an answer to prayer. St. Paul tells us he prayed that his fellow Christians would be "filled with the knowledge of his [God's] will in spiritual wisdom and understanding" (Colossians 1:9). He was praying, I take it, for discernment. For what is spiritual wisdom but the power to make sound judgments about spiritual things? Spiritual wisdom helps us decide when to speak and when to keep silent, when to act and when to wait, when to fight and when to surrender. Spiritual wisdom — fallible and subjective — is the power to know what is really going on when others are camouflaging the issues. And it is the power to know what is really going on inside our own hearts. The Bible tells us our hearts are very deceitful (Jeremiah 17:9), and not even love makes them wholly trustworthy. Hence, what we need in the life of love is the gift of discernment, or spiritual wisdom. For this we can only pray; when it is given, we must use it boldly.

In the kingdom of God self-denying love will work in perfect harmony with justice. We will not need to demand our own rights, for others will, in love's discernment, recognize and give us our rights. We will not need to sacrifice our rights in order to protect the rights of others because their rights will be honored by all. But we do not yet live in God's perfect community.

We desperately need the power of agapic love. With it, we have spiritual insight into the needs of other people. With it, we have power to get above our own selfish preoccupation with our own rights to where we can recognize the rights of others. With it we can do the amazingly loving thing, forsaking our own rights for the sake of other people's rights. As we have seen, the rights of others in our world can often best be served if we demand our rights. This reality is one basic limit to love's sublime indifference to its own rights. But the hope of life is the fact that the redemptive power of love does move within the complex arrangements of rights and claims. And this power is the only power within reality that moves people to sacrifice their own rights for the sake of the needs of others.

6
Love Does Not Seek Its Own Self

LOVE DOES NOT SEEK its own, the song says. In the preceding chapter we talked about seeking and sacrificing our rights. This time, translate that line as: "Love does not seek its own self." Love is the power that moves us to seek others. This being true, love appears to resist one of the deepest drives within any healthy being — the drive to discover and become one's own ideal self. At our best do we not all want to be one with the self we are meant to be? Do we not all, in this profound sense, want to seek ourselves? How can divine love be opposed to every person's most important adventure in life, his search for his own self?

Self-seeking, in its best sense, is not merely tolerated as a petty vice; it is urged on us as our highest duty. Aristotle called it self-realization; he said that persons are most moral when they seek to realize their selves. In our time Erich Fromm has told us that our highest calling is precisely to "take loving care of ourselves." Self-seeking is our humanistic duty. If he is right, most of us are doing very well morally: the one thing we want to do is take care of ourselves and become our true selves. We train our children to be self-seekers, and we feel most successful as parents when our children manage well in self-seeking. Indeed, we usually feel we are on God's side especially when we are searching hardest for our true selves.

Yet we who live under the influence of Jesus Christ are confronted with another call — the call of self-denying love. Jesus' own sacrificial life puts all of our self-seeking into question. His words throw our humanistic aspirations into doubt: "If anyone wants to be my disciple, let him *deny* himself. . . ." And even when we forget his words, we feel the power of love within us, nudging us toward care for others and forgetfulness of ourselves. Self-denial and self-seeking seem to be on a collision course: to follow love you must deny yourself and to seek yourself you must deny agapic love.

Must God's self-giving love and our self-seeking needs cancel each other out? Are they uncompromising enemies? It is hard for us to settle for unrelieved hostility between Christian love and human self-seeking. Divine love sets our humanist search for self under a shadow, but does it prevent every kind of self-seeking? In this chapter, we shall see that love not only allows but requires us to seek ourselves — on one condition. We shall also see that self-seeking on its own traps us into a horrible tyranny, and that love alone can liberate us from it.

What do we seek?

What is it that we seek when we seek ourselves? We seek two things — our own identity and our fulfilment; to know who we really are and to become what we really are. We probably cannot do one without the other. Becoming our true selves depends on knowing who we really are, and we cannot really know who we are until we become what we truly are.

1. We seek self-knowledge. Know yourself! From earliest time this has been the aim of all human understanding. We cannot be at peace with ourselves until we know who we really are. Our frenetic fumbling for self-knowledge exposes our anxiety that we do not know ourselves. Sociologists use the word *anomie* for this widespread loss of a sense for who we are. *Anomie* is the feeling of dangling in the spiritual winds, unattached to the institutions, traditions, and norms that used to give people a quiet feeling for who they are, where they come from, and to whom they belong — mostly without thinking about it much. We think about nothing as much as we do about ourselves. So we seek ourselves in many places. We seek ourselves in our roots — looking to where we came from. We seek ourselves in counseling and therapy — looking for the selves reflected in our feelings or our subconscious. We seek ourselves in religion — looking for a revelation of our identity through a prophetic word or a mystic illumination. We seek ourselves in groups — looking for a reflection of what we are in other people's responses to us. Wherever we seek, our quest is painful, frustrating, and unending, but one thing remains clear: to know ourselves is the one thing needful. We cannot believe that love would resist our urge to know who we really are.

2. We seek to become ourselves. Become yourself! This is the goal of every person awake to his or her own potential. The quest for the self we can be and yet are not is a form of self-seeking that pushes us toward an ideal. It is the drive to bridge the gulf between what we are and what we are meant to be. Some psychologists have called this search for the self the "actualizing tendency" in human beings; it is our bent for bringing all that we are potentially into the reality of our actual lives. The ancients were aware of this "actualizing tendency" and made it the base for our highest moral duty — the duty to realize, to make real, our own potential as human beings. This kind of self-seeking appeals to the brightest and noblest within us.

We are not talking here about the mean sort of selfishness often associated with self-seeking. We must suppose that God's love song is saying something more profound and provocative than the obvious truth that agapic love is not selfish in that sense, that it does not push us to claw and scramble over fallen bodies to the winner's circle. Obviously, the love displayed in the cross of Christ does not drive us to relentless grabbing for our own pleasure and profit in total disregard of the rights and needs of others. The contradiction between agapic love and gross scrambling for self-satisfaction is obvious: love is not selfish. We have to ask further whether love also cancels out the self-seeking of the noble soul — the seeking for the ideal self we have yet to find and yet to become.

"Love does not seek its own." Shall we sing this only as an ecstatic exaggeration, against the grain of what we know in our hearts, a pious, romantic lyric meant to be sung, not acted out? We feel at our moral best precisely when we strive to become more of our better self than we are. And when we feel we have attained a glimmer of our best self, we think of it as a gift of God. How deep is this need! How strong is this drive! How tragic when we lose it and come to terms too soon with the self we usually are. How, then, can we sing: "love does not seek its own?"

There is a simple answer, I believe, though it is not easy to practice. The answer is this: our self can be either a *means* or an *end*. If we make our self the *end*, the ultimate goal, the final aim of our striving, we are in conflict with agapic love. Love does not seek its self as the living end. Instead love is the power that drives us to seek our selves as a *means* to being agents of love. This will take some thinking through; and it is very important to get it straight. If we do not have it clear, we will never relieve our conflict between self-seeking and self-denial.

We must separate end from means.

First consider what happens when we make our selves the *end* or goal of our seeking. Self becomes the supreme good. Our ideal self becomes the standard for judging everything that happens to us and everything we do. If the self we seek as the end of life is the commercialized model of success, power, and wealth which contemporary materialism urges on us, we size up people brutally and crudely. But whenever the self is the ultimate, we tend to see other people as instruments for our growth. Even when our ideal self is noble and good, we are inclined to evaluate people in terms of how they can help us in our climb towards our ideal self. Indeed, when our ideal is the sanctified self, the morally good self, we tend to assess our relationships with people by this standard: how can this contact, acquaintance, friendship contribute to my drive to become the ideal person?

The source of all the evils connected with self-seeking is that we turn our ideal self into an idol and expect other people to dance around it. We come to think our idol excuses everything. We exploit people and push them around, lie to them, flatter them, put them down. Whether crudely or with artistic finesse, we treat them as replaceable supports for the ego we are trying to build into a self. This is the poison that so easily gets into all erotic love; we love others only so that they will be acolytes at the altar of our divinized self.

The image of the self that is sought as the idol of ultimate devotion takes on different and changing forms. The ideal self of immature people is a fabric woven of fads and fancies. For others, more mature and yet not fully developed, the ideal is the productive self. For others, it is a mixture of the noble, wise, humane saint and the earthy, happy sinner. For still others, the model is Jesus of Nazareth. A composite portrait of the typical secular ideal self, as portrayed in the escapist literature, television, and film of our day, would disclose a combination of all that is creative, charming, clever, and courageous. Such a person is healthy and vital, good-looking, sexually interesting but capable of deep caring. Not only does this ideal person know much, he or she has the wit to express it vividly. Confident yet not arrogant, religious, yet not other-worldly, this ideal is strong against temptation, but understanding of those who yield. When he or she loves, it is always from strength. This is a frame into which most of our ideal selves fit; each of us makes a private portrait by adding a few unique features.

Many people combine a kind of self-denial with self-worship. Self-denial of this sort says No only to *things*; it is really self-discipline. We exercise even if we hate doing it; we do not smoke; we turn down the rich food we love to eat; we deny ourselves for the sake of a healthy body. We work seven days a week; we enroll in university courses; we give up movies, television, and socializing in order to become more productive. We resist sexual temptation; we turn down un-ethical financial opportunities; we exercise our wills in order to become morally better.

All these sorts of denials have in common that they are disciplines, not self-denials. They are denials of things, not a denial of the self. Their spiritual value depends wholly on one question: are they for the self as an end, or for the self as a means of love?

We have said enough about seeking our selves as the be-all and end-all of life. It is now clear that love could not seek its own self as life's ultimate goal. Now we must go on to ask how love might drive us to seek our selves not as an end but as a means. Why does love move us to seek our selves as an agent of love?

Love is the divine force that moves us to make the neighbor our center of concern, drives us toward him without demanding a reward. Love does not put the self on center stage and ask the world around to applaud. Love does not praise a neighbor only to get praise in return. Love does not strive to become the better self merely to enjoy the excitement of being a splendid person. Love lifts our sights beyond the ideal self we are seeking. For this reason, not even our ideal self is our god, the goal of our life's quest. Hence, love cannot be self-seeking unless the self being sought is pre-registered as an agent of love.

Precisely because love has to have effective agents, it is at peace with self-seeking. Love *needs* a kind of self-seeking for the sake of the neighbor whom we love.

Love needs self-seeking.

Consider a few reasons why love requires us to seek ourselves.

1. Agapic love takes a lot of energy. It requires considerable physical and psychic vitality to love a person without the promise of the rewards we all seek from love. To love a husband or a wife, a lover, a son or a daughter, or a friend well sometimes takes more vigor than we can muster; to love a mere neighbor takes far more. Prodigious amounts of energy are consumed when we keep on doing the works of love without reasonable return in the form of affection, praise, or even credit with God. Some people cannot manage loving well, not because they do not want to, but because they are not in good shape. To be in loving condition for the rigors of agape, we need to be physically and spiritually fit.

2. *Love must do its work now through the reality of our actual selves.* Love cannot wait until we find and become our ideal selves. For this reason, our self-seeking must also take the form of a search for and an acceptance of our real selves. We cannot love well if we are forever locked into a losing argument with the imperfect reality of what we are. Our actual selves *are* in many respects limited and blemished. In part we are the sorts of people we are because of the combination of genes we inherited from our parents. We are limited by the consequences of profound childhood experiences, many of which we have forgotten or suppressed. Our humanity limits us: we are neither gods nor angels. We carry within us a heritage of moral and spiritual failure as part of our invisible baggage. If we feel we must love with the energy of an angel, the vision of a prophet, the intellectual power of a genius, and the virtue of a saint, we will be frustrated lovers.

The demands of ideal selfhood are too much for our actual selves. If we accept them, we will be dragged down by them; we will not be able to endure them. And we will seek escape. We may not be tempted to commit suicide — though that temptation is not unusual. Mostly we wish we could evaporate somehow, and magically reappear in a place where all the pressures disappear as the fog with the rise of the morning sun. But one of the victims of that kind of escapism is love. We cannot love well when what we want most is to escape love's demands. So love moves us to seek again for our actual selves, with all their limits, to accept them and with them begin anew our quest of the more loving self.

3. *Agapic love requires the art of loving.* Bungling can ruin the works of love. Romantic love, we all know, needs a delicate art to be all that we want it to be; ecstasy does not come without preparation. Agapic love needs artistry even more urgently. Gestures of love are often refused because they are botched by clumsy lovers. We can frighten people by our tactless advances into their lives. Love that is too persistent can burden people: many needful persons want to be helped and then left alone after love's work is finished. Patronizing attitudes accompanying works of love can intimidate people; showy piety can offend them.

Love requires us to seek a self that is wise, discreet, and politic, so that it can do its work through us. Effective love is as much an art as it is a good intention, and like all art, it comes with hard work, persistent seeking for our most effective selves.

Agapic love, to sum up, moves us to reject the humanist search for our ideal self as our life's ultimate goal, but it empowers us to seek ourselves as agents of effective love. Having seen this point very clearly, we may finish this chapter by observing how love not only *opposes* making a god of the ideal self, but *liberates* us from this god. And by liberating us from the false god of the ideal self, love enables us to find ourselves as real agents of love.

Love gives us freedom from self-seeking.

The ideal self is an intolerant self. It will never forgive us for failing to be in reality what we ought ideally to be. Indeed, it *cannot* forgive us, for it is only a fantasy which we have turned into a demanding idol.

What makes matters worse is that most of us are uncertain as to what our ideal self is really like. Models are thrown at us from the media, from popular psychology, and from pulpits. Is the ideal self the assertive self? or the sexy self? or the affluent self? or the powerful self? or perhaps the self of moral virtue? Maybe it is a composite of all these. Unsure, we bow frantically to them all.

The many images that clamor to be our ideal selves confuse our search, producing ever deeper anxiety for anyone who wants above everything else to be all that his or her ideal self demands. Anxiety, in turn, is deepened by the many obstacles to finding ourselves. We are frustrated by physical weakness, from stomach cramps to heart attacks. We are held back by our own laziness and lusts. And death always stands by to terminate our search before we get it well underway. We have little time and much weakness. How could we even fantasize becoming the ideal person? Meanwhile the elusive idol of our ideal self drives us mercilessly. The humanistic goal becomes a demonic tyrant. It is the essence of what St. Paul called the commandment that promises life but kills us in the end (Romans 7:10).

In the face of such frustration, we have two options. We can let the ideal defeat us, and force us into quiet despair and secret guilt, even while we get on with the ordinary business of living. Or we can accept our real selves, far removed from the ideal, and live lovingly through these limited and warped and blemished selves. The second option comes only as a gift of love. Love liberates us from the idol of our ideal selves. It does not deny that there is an ideal self; it only refuses to move us to seek it as an ultimate goal.

Love liberates us from the idol, in the first place, by letting us see that the ideal self does not have to be the one thing we need to become. It convinces us that God accepts our actual self in forgiveness and adoption as his children. God's love, then, shows us that our actual, blemished self is the only self that can be an agent of love. In the second place, love liberates us from the ideal self as idol by showing that the ideal self can and will be handled by God. Jesus Christ is the model of our ideal self; he is what we are meant to be. And God will lead us to that self in his own time. He will take care of our becoming the self we seek to be. That is, love itself will *give* us the ideal self; no wonder that love does not need to seek its own self as the ultimate goal in life.

Love's liberation allows us to regard our ideal self with a sense of humor. We can strive with God's help to be a better self, to become more of our ideal, our true, Christian self. But moved by love we will not be overly serious about it. Indeed, once love knocks the idol down and we see it as a false god, we can even have a good laugh at it — and at ourselves for being taken in by it. We know that the only purpose for seeking our ideal selves is to become better at seeking others. And we, in love, can now seek others with the real selves we are. We can seek others the better, in fact, the more we leave the ideal self with God and let love move us the way we are.

7
Love Is Not Irritable

LOVE, THE POET TELLS US, is not irritable. That is good news, because irritability, while no great sin, is certainly a spiritual nuisance. And sometimes it is a major menace. The wrong button in the hands of an irritable general could produce a holocaust. But even if it accomplished no more than the prevention of ulcers, love's power to arrest irritability in the hearts of people would be worthy of a celebration.

What is it like to be irritable? Irritability is the emotional launching pad for anger. To be irritable is to be in a constant countdown for a temperamental blast-off. It is to have your insides coiled, ready to spring into fury. The spiritual membranes of an irritable person are inflamed; the slightest friction sends a surge of pain through his system.

What is it like, then, to be angry? Anger comes in many models and wears a thousand disguises, so we cannot draw a simple picture. But we know that anger is an emotion, even a kind of passion. And it brings pain; anger makes us scream and sometimes cry because of the pain. But anger is also energy. An angry person wants to tear things apart. Unlike sadness, which is heavy and immobile, anger pushes us into attack.

What do we *do* when we get angry? We throw a tantrum. We cry. We spit out four-letter words. We fight. Or we put our anger under a lid and hide it from ourselves because we are ashamed to see it. Perhaps we disguise it; we pass it off as sadness, regret, sympathy, or any of a hundred different emotions that seem more respectable to us than anger. If we are in good spiritual shape, we communicate our anger; we admit it to ourselves and to those at whom we are angry. What we do with anger usually depends on the sorts of persons we are.

What can we realistically expect the power of love to do with our irritability? Let us make sure, at the beginning, that we do not expect love to take away our *capacity* for anger. Anyone who cannot get angry is immobilized by fear; he is not sensitized by love. The love song does not say that love never gets angry. It says that love does not get angry very easily. Love puts a long fuse on our emotional bombs. It can be provoked, but not easily.

We do not want Christian love to turn us into spineless souls without heat or passion. We want the freedom to get angry, but we want freedom from slavery to our anger. We want to calm the furies within us and overcome our taut and ugly susceptibility to quick anger. We want to conquer irritability, not anger.

How does agapic love reduce irritability? We have to have a diagnosis of the disease before we can understand the remedy. Once we know what it is that makes us irritable, we may be able to see how love works as an antidote.

Why are we irritable?

The basic cause of irritability is erotic love. Erotic love is the root of irritability because it is personal power generated by personal need. We reach out and strive for anything that promises to satisfy our deep desires to be complete human beings. Whether it is the need for security or intimacy or eternal happiness, we grasp for whatever promises to give it to us. We strive toward friends, and lovers, and parents, and God, always in the nervous hope that they will satisfy us when we get close to them. This restless reaching beyond ourselves is what has through the ages been called love. It is erotic love and in it are the seeds of irritability.

Erotic love is the root of irritability because our pursuit of fulness always falls short of the perfect ending. There is always something that frustrates our grasp for happiness. We are frustrated most in our self-propelled quest to be in tune with God. But countless smaller things frustrate us along the way. A baby is frustrated when its mother forces it to use a toilet. An adolescent's desire to be attractive is frustrated by acne. A young woman feels thwarted if destiny leaves her with a flat chest. A husband is frustrated by his wife's frigidity or by her aggressive demand for equality. A wife is frustrated by her husband's failure as a lover or provider. Men and women are frustrated in their competition for jobs and, once they land a job, by its tedium or by their employer's failure to appreciate their work enough. These are all irritants. But are they the sorts of things that make us irritable? Or do they irritate us as much as they do because we are *already* irritable? There is more here than meets the eye.

Where do we get the idea that there must be more to life than we have found? Why do we never stop dreaming of a full life? Why are we never satisfied? The answer is *eros*. Eros is the restless human drive for happiness and completeness. The urge comes from the abyss of our souls. At its deepest, it is the urge for God, profoundly and memorably expressed in Augustine's confession "Our hearts are restless, until they find their rest in thee." We would not be far wrong to translate Augustine's words: "We are irritable, O Lord, until we make our peace with you."

Our failure to find peace with God is the ultimate reason that every inconvenience turns into an irritant. We do not *feel* our irritability in our religious life. We feel it in the concrete irritations of ordinary life. The reason so many things irritate us is that, out of tune with God, we miss the power of agapic love. Lacking that, we make our unfilled ego the axis around which we want the world to turn. Beginning with our parents, but soon taking in our siblings, our friends, our lovers, our spouses, and finally our children, we turn everyone within our orbit into a provider of our erotic needs. But the world will not always revolve around our ego, and so even the smallest frustration can become an irritant. This is because unfulfilled eros has already made us irritable.

Irritability has consequences in our life.

Irritability makes us prone to anger, robs us of joy, and pushes us toward hostility. Let us look more closely at each of these shock waves set in motion by the clash between life's longings and life's frustrations.

1. Anger. Being irritable, we are bound often to be angry people. None of us escapes. We get angry at every small obstacle that slows us down or gets in our way. We grind our teeth if we are sixth in line at a checkout counter and someone ahead is having a leisurely conversation with the checker. We rage if a bolt seems to be missing from a toy that needs to be assembled before Christmas. We fume if a waitress ignores us when we have only half an hour for lunch. We are furious if a teen-age son or daughter promises to be home with the car by midnight and keeps us up waiting until two in the morning. We are in a pique if dinner is late two nights running and tasteless to boot. Behind these fleeting irritants lie far deeper frustrations, buried in our hidden memories. And behind these is the deepest of all — the frustration of not being the fulfilled, happy, complete person we were meant to be. We have a great supply of frustrations. Compacted within us, they create an intense potential for anger.

2. Loss of joy. Joy is the experience of gratitude. We have it now and then, sometimes even over long periods. At those moments when we feel life coming to us as a sheer gift — undeserved, unearned, magnificently free — we feel joy. Irritability robs us of joy because it is a sense of frustration over not getting what we think we deserve. We are irritable because we are frustrated in our sweating, grunting scramble for satisfaction. The more we strive, the higher we reach, the greater our frustrations. Our agitated souls lose their awareness of life as a gift. We cannot feel gratitude for life as a gift when we feel cheated out of the life we are trying to earn. This is painful. It is the loss of joy.

3. Hostility. Hostility is anger turned aggressive. When anger makes us hostile, we want to cut and thrust at the target of our anger. We see the person we are angry with as an enemy. But we do not want to make peace by resolving the offense. We want to keep the quarrel going.

If we are civilized enough, we may limit the conflict to words. Sometimes we will lash out with a frontal verbal assault: "I was furious that you forgot our luncheon appointment yesterday." But to be even more cutting, we may launch the attack from the side, in the form of sarcasm and innuendo: "Well, now, that was typically considerate of you not to come by for lunch yesterday." But sarcasm only deepens our hostility. The hostile person wants to destroy. Therein lies the danger of hostility: it is the next step toward violence.

Violence, like anger, is rooted deeply in irritability. But before an irritable person turns to violence, he is likely to have been terribly frustrated and fiercely hostile. Somebody frustrates him, makes him feel helpless, and so becomes an enemy that must be hurt. No parent becomes a child-beater merely because of irritability. A parent becomes a child-beater only if he or she is deeply hostile towards others — perhaps a parent, perhaps a spouse, but always himself or herself. When the child frustrates the parent, and there is no relief from it, the irritation can trigger not only anger but violence. No husband beats a wife merely because he is irritable; he beats his wife because his angry emotions have been left to sear his spirit over a long time, long enough for them to turn into hostility. And then, when frustrations come, he turns to violence. Hostility and violence are possible only because we have become irritable.

Let us summarize. Irritability is a spiritual readiness to get angry. We become irritated for countless specific reasons. We discover that we are irritable when irritants smack us. But the single, deepest cause of our irritability is our frustrated need for the satisfaction of being a fulfilled, complete person. Being irritable is not a sin; but it is the inevitable result of being a sinful creature trying to grow into maturity and fulness. But being irritable is a possible menace, for it robs us of joy and it can always spread into hostility.

Now we must ask what agapic love does with irritability.

Some things agapic love does not do for irritability.

1. *Agape does not disguise anger.* It is possible to avoid the problem of irritability by disguising our anger. By making believe we are not angry, we may be able to maintain the pretense that we are not inwardly anger-prone. If we suspect that it is wicked to be angry, we can twist our feelings into other moods that seem more acceptable. Thus we try for the best of both worlds. We give signals to other people that they have done something that deserves anger, but that we are too good to get angry. This gives us the luxury of expressing anger without the risk of having it thrown back at us. Besides, we can thereby arouse guilt feelings in others and get them to feel they owe us something.

If our children leave their rooms in a mess after being told several times to clean them up, we can clean them ourselves, always with a sigh and a groan, always so that they can see us. We thus let our anger parade as hurt goodness. Our reward is the illusion that the children will then recognize how much they owe us for being such sacrificing, longsuffering parents. A woman is angry at her family for forcing her into a domestic mold that does not satisfy her. So she throws herself into housework with a self-righteous vengeance. After all, she feels, what right has she to be angry at having to do what every woman was created to do? So she disguises her anger with a mask of grim and joyless dedication to the housekeeper's role, and she expects to be praised and loved for her sacrifice.

Disguising anger relieves other people of the responsibility of doing something about our anger. But it forces them to cope with an irritable *person*, who will not let his or her anger be recognized for what it is. And the disguises behind which life is lived in painful anger only prevent us from changing the situation that causes the real anger. The upshot is that we become even more irritable.

2. *Agape does not unleash anger.* There are more ways than one to express anger. It is possible to unleash it on the world untamed, to ventilate it willy-nilly. We can cut and thrust at everyone and everything that frustrates us in the smallest way. This is as dangerous as disguised anger. In a sense it may be healthy for the person expressing it, but it leaves hurt and bleeding people in its wake. Paul may have had such indiscriminate expression of anger in mind when he said, "Be angry, but do not sin" (Ephesians 4:26). He may have been saying: "Do not disguise your anger, but do not let it roam the streets unleashed either."

3. *Agape does not remove irritants from our lives.* If divine love possessed everyone in our environment, we might be free of irritants. But love does not fully possess anyone in our experience. So love does not take away people who have the potential to irritate us.

People irritate us by rubbing our sensitive egos. They do not appreciate us. They ignore us when we need to be noticed. They remind us of duty when we want to have fun. They do not respond when we cry for help. And they are more successful than we are, though they have fewer talents than we.

People even irritate us by their love. Love is often put in clumsy hands. Love belabored is boring love. There is a well-meant love that chokes us; people push into our lives and cling to us with love when we want to be left alone. I have known people on deathbeds whose dying was made more miserable by loving people who would not leave them alone.

4. *Agape does not reduce irritability by forbidding anger.* Agapic love does not overcome our irritability by persuading us that we should not be irritable. We have seen that love is effective as a law only when it first works as power. Knowing that we ought to love and knowing that love is not irritable, we are tempted to think, "I ought to love, so I had better stop being irritable and start feeling more loving." But that only makes matters worse by preparing us for more frustration. We

cannot *make* ourselves feel loving in the agapic sense. And if we try because we are commanded, we will only become the more irritable as people and things cross our paths to prevent us from feeling loving.

To forbid all anger in the name of love is as mistaken as forbidding someone to be irritable. Love does not make anger wrong. There are things in life that demand our getting angry at them. Not to feel anger at them would mean we are either insensitive to evil or afraid to feel anger. We would be in a moral stupor if we failed to get angry at racial injustice and the hunger of children. We would be less than human if we failed to get angry at pain and the loss of precious things in our own lives. Jeremiah was seething when he said, "I am full of the wrath of the Lord; I am weary of holding it in" (Jeremiah 6:11). Jesus was furious with the Pharisees. And God's anger was kindled against Israel time and again, often enough to make him appear to be a very irritable God. Love does not forbid anger.

What does agapic love do to reduce irritability?

Generally speaking, we may say that agapic love has the power to reduce irritability because it is the power to turn the direction of our desire towards the needs of other people. As we have noted earlier, it is the power to relate to other people's needs without demanding a return on our investment. Since we are not reaching out only for self-fulfilment and happiness, we will not feel frustration as sharply and painfully as we do when personal satisfaction is the exclusive goal of our lives. Let us look in more detail at some ways this works.

1. Agapic love reduces irritability because it meets our deepest need. There is no way to experience the power of agape without experiencing God himself. This is the point John makes persistently: "If we love one another, God abides in us and his love is perfected in us. . . . God is love, and he who abides in love abides in God, and God abides in him" (1 John 4:12, 16). Love is so close to God's very being that when we receive love we receive God himself. God lives in anyone who lives in love. This brings about a union between two persons who are meant for each other. And the person of God in union with us gives the ultimate answer to our erotic desires. It comes as a gift. Our restless search for the completion of life in God comes to its first, though not perfect, fulfilment as soon as we experience the love of God as a gift.

2. Agapic love reduces the potential for frustration. Agapic love dethrones self-satisfaction as the ruling monarch of our lives. Once satisfying our own deepest desires is less than our ultimate goal, love begins to reduce our irritability by thrusting our energies in the direction of the needs and rights of other people. Agape does not take away the needs that eros seeks to satisfy nor reduce the number of things that frustrate us, but we no longer *feel* the frustrations in the same way. We do not feel as vexed, stirred up, agitated by things when we are concerned about others as when we are only concerned about ourselves. I have seen medical doctors in the situation of caring for patients and in the situation of being a patient. Caring for patients, the doctor is able to absorb without getting ruffled the annoyance of people who are surly, stupid, and unresponsive to his care. When the same doctor is ill, concerned about his own health, he becomes irritated at the slightest hint that he is not being properly cared for. The psychodynamics of this are complex, but it is clear that a shift of concern from self to others reduces irritation.

3. Agapic love gives power to communicate anger. The power of love gives us the freedom to admit that we are angry and to express our anger constructively. This is not merely a freedom to sound off, lose our tempers, and go into a tantrum. The freedom to communicate our anger to others is not a license to hurt them, but freedom to change the situation that causes anger.

Love's power comes to us first as a gift received. We feel first the freedom of being loved powerfully. God's unconditional love gives us freedom to know how anger-prone we are, to admit to ourselves that we are angry people. We can admit our anger to ourselves and express it to others because we can accept ourselves as anger-prone persons.

If we can admit to ourselves and others that we are angry, we lose all reason to disguise our anger in the garb of false concern or pretended sweetness. And we do not need to use anger to force the other person's hand. When we ventilate our anger without love in the face of another person, we are really trying to force him into making a response that we need. We may want him to grovel and melt into abject guilt. Or we may want him to tremble before our anger and do what we want him to do. Or we express our anger to force him to get angry back at us, so that we can have it out and become worse enemies than before, thus justifying our anger twofold. We do this because we really want to hang on to our irritability.

Acting in the freedom of agapic love, our object will be to change the situation we are angry about. But we will let the person we are angry at be free to respond to our anger as he can and will. If he acts forgivingly, so much the better; if he acts angrily and unforgivingly, we will nonetheless leave him free to make the response he is able to make, trusting that at another time and in another situation, he may change his feelings.

4. Agapic love increases gratitude. Agapic love is the power to overcome irritability because it is the power to see life as a gift. God comes to us as freely as the wind; once having come, he opens our eyes to a new world. It is a new world to us because we see it in a new way. No longer is the world around us an obstacle course we must run to achieve our reward of happiness. Our environment is not a maze that we must puzzle out successfully or be damned forever. The world is a gift, a playground where we discover our very selves as gifts of God. The first breath of the morning, the first handshake from a friend, the first "good morning" from a spouse, the chance to be healthy, the opportunity to work — all of it a gift from God!

This is not sloppy romanticism. We know all about the shadows — the agony and the misery. Some people are being robbed of their rights, and some are starving, and life for some is worse than death. The fact remains that when we are given the power to be concerned about other people's miseries and needs, we will feel our own lives as gifts; and this opens the windows of gratitude.

Gratitude is an antidote to irritability. We cannot be coiled for anger as long as we are feeling grateful for life. The barrage of irritants that besets us will not throw us into a spate of vexation. Frustration will not undo us and spin us into paroxysms of anger. How can we be on the edge of fury when we are feeling the wonder that we should exist at all?

* * *

Before ending this chapter, I want to repeat the very crucial point. We must not suppose that a taste of agapic love today will sweep away every tendency to get angry. It will not, for two reasons. First, agapic love does not unravel a lifetime of irritability at once. The inflammation of the ego takes a long time to heal. Second, we need to get angry, and we need the ability for rage. Agapic love, in fact, will move us to anger at things that leave a person cold who is driven only by a need to satisfy himself. Things that do not touch us directly may infuriate us because they frustrate our brothers and sisters in their move for justice. With agapic love we will be given a new power for anger, but at the same time we will be amazed at our tolerance for annoyances that used to drive us up the wall because they blocked our way to pleasure and fulfilment.

8
Love Is Not Resentful

RESENTMENT IS YESTERDAY'S irritation scratched into the sensitive membranes of our memory. It is yesterday's hurt grown up into today's indignation. Planted and tended in our memory, the thorn that first pricked us now stabs away at our peace. Memories of minor hurts become major resentments.

Any evil once done is an everlasting fact. In a sense everything we do lasts forever. Pilate's copout goes on forever. Peter's denial reverberates through the corridors of time. Our petty sins and major deceits echo on. And one indication of the everlastingness of our actions is memory, our personal share in the living past. Resentment is our memory of the painful, angry past.

Why do we take the past into our minds and lock it there to keep it alive? Why do we prolong the hurts we receive instead of remembering only the joys of the past? We remember the hurts so that we can *enjoy* the pain of yesterday over and over again. We keep it alive for the pleasure we can get from our resentment against the one who hurts us.

Love alone has the power to release memory's grip on yesterday's evil, for only love is the power that moves us toward people without expectation of return and therefore with a great tolerance for hurt. Love does not demand explanations and apologies or keep accounts. Love does not take pleasure in remembering how much we have coming from people who hurt us. For love is the power whose only direction is the help, healing, and salvation of the other person. This is why love has the power to overcome resentment.

To understand this dimension of love's power, we must take a longer look at resentment.

Resentment brings us deadly pleasures.

Resentment is bittersweet. If we did not cherish it, we would let it go. What sort of rewards do we get from our resentment? Why do we keep score? First, it makes us feel superior to the person we resent. Also, it gives us an excuse for indulging in exquisite plots for revenge, such as hurting the person by withholding our ultimate treasure — personal friendship. The more power we have the more dangerous is this kind of resentment. Third, there is a sense in which we want to remember past wounds to hurt ourselves. But, of course, we chew the cud of past wrongs to *enjoy* the feeling of hurt that the memory rekindles. How we fondle these memories. We savor them lying in bed when we cannot sleep; we mull over them while driving our car; we brood over them while listening to sermons on love. We play the tape again and again because we get a strange, distorted pleasure in being hurt again — like someone who cannot keep his tongue off a sensitive tooth. We not only enjoy the painful pleasure of remembered hurt, we also enjoy feeling *noble* and *worthy* as the decent person who was wrongly hurt. Resentments serve a double purpose: they give us treasured pain and they give us a chance to justify ourselves. So we get two rewards — neurotic pleasure and religious pride.

But we do, in fact, also hate resentment. We hate it because we are miserable in it. It depresses us, robs us of gratitude, sneaks into other relationships. Resentment left to fester against an individual sours our relations with our wives, our children, and our mutual friends. We have a love-hate relationship with our own resentments. But, most important, we are helpless to deal with resentment, to *forget* — unless we yield to the power of love, the power, that is, of the Spirit of Christ.

Resentment is deadly because its target is persons. We do not merely remember the hurtful thing done; we keep a finely tuned focus on the person who did it. The memory of an evil *action* merely summons the will to undo it and set it right, but the memory of a person who hurt us inflames a feeling of hostility toward that person, isolating him from our care and exiling him from our life. As far as his life relates to ours, it puts him in a cancer ward, a spiritual incurable. We can do nothing for him or with him until love breaks down our resentment.

Resentment forces a neighbor to be and remain an enemy. As we insist on keeping score of hurts, resentment feeds our anxiety that we are behind in this game of ill-will and must catch up. Resentment keeps enemy lists, files on every person who has injured us. Each one must pay for the pain he caused before he can face us as a moral equal.

Resentment is doubly deadly because it views the real person, whose fault is being kept alive, through a lens fouled by anger. Irritated by a person, we slice his single offense from the whole picture of what he is and from all the good and decent things he has done. We insulate ourselves from feeling any obligation to remember his needs. Pushing everything else into the backwaters of our feelings, we frame that single wrong vividly, intensely, painfully in our memory. This is how resentment justifies our refusal to love by falsifying reality. We force our memory to distort reality so we can justify irrational resentment.

We want the offending person to remember the wrong as clearly as we do, so that when we finally even the score, he will be hurt enough to satisfy us. Resentment is really a painful desire that the other person feel a pain he knows he deserves.

We have even more complicated reasons for not wanting others to forget. Suppose that it was you who once caused hurt to someone, and that the person you hurt has kept the memory of that alive for years. He has woven a tangled web of resentment against you. You have felt it, obliquely and subtly but acutely. You have sensed sudden coldness in his voice; you have felt left out of intimate circles; you have detected a studied reserve in your relationship. You have, in short, felt his anger without explanation, rejection without confrontation. His resentment has hurt you just as it has been hurting him. He lets your hurtful act fester in his mind; you let his refusal to forgive fester in your mind.

One day a chance encounter opens the door to a possible reconciliation. He makes a gesture, an awkward, cumbersome, half-spoken move toward reconciliation. He wants only to begin where you both are with a new relationship, leaving the past in the limbo of canceled memories. But your own resentment is too fresh. You want the whole record laid out on the table, nothing short of a stenographer's transcription of what each said and did. The mean and painful past must be clear in everyone's head before it can be done with. Why? Why does our resentment — aimed now at the other person's resentment — have this terrible urge to force everyone to relive the past?

There is only one reason. We need to justify ourselves. We must be sure that everyone involved knows that the other person's resentments were unjustified, all out of proportion to the wrong of our original offense. It must be clear to all that *we* are the morally superior one.

This is how we often deal with family grudges. A woman confronts her husband for having offended her at a party. In a few minutes, he is demanding that she recall, word for word, the time she belittled him in front of friends — two years before. He has remembered and resented. Now he demands that she also remember. Why does he do this? Because he needs to know that she knows what the virtue score is. He will not let his petty offense put her in first place in the "Who's the better person?" contest. Once he knows that she knows that his offense tonight was smaller than her two-year-old put-down, he may be able to admit his wrong and cancel his case against her. She cannot win because his resentment is too strong. In fact, of course, neither will win — for next week's slipup by one or the other will call for the same sort of hateful scorekeeping. Resentment, a minor vice? It is one of the deadliest known to man. The irony is that it always kills the spirit of the person who wields it.

Love exorcises resentment.

But now comes our song to say that love drives out the demon of remembered pain. How does love drive away the painful memories we so ardently harbor? Only agape has the power. To understand agape's power we compare it again with eros. Erotic love always keeps score, nourishing old wounds and remembering old hurts. For eros is born of powerful personal need, and our drive to satisfy such enormous need is often thwarted. Eros thwarted is eros hurt. Erotic hurt is so intense that we cannot help remembering having our love spurned or abused. Have you ever heard of a jilted lover who forgot the person who jilted him?

The power of agapic love drives us to a new beginning. Love lets the past die. It moves people to a new beginning *without* settling the past. Love does not have to clear up all misunderstandings. In its power, the details of the past become irrelevant; only its new beginning matters. Accounts may go unsettled; differences remain unsolved; ledgers stay unbalanced. Conflicts between people's memories of how things happened are not cleared up; the past stays muddled. Only the future matters. Love's power does not make fussy historians. Love prefers to tuck all the loose ends of past rights and wrongs in the bosom of forgiveness — and pushes us into a new start. Letting go of the past and beginning here, now, where we are, to move again toward a reconciled life is one of the hardest things any human being is ever asked to do. Love is the power to do that.

God's love is our model. It keeps coming to us though we have fed a thousand offenses into his memory-bank. God's love is also our power. We are enabled by a love that keeps no accounts since they were settled by Christ at his cross. From the cross, God moves on to new history. He does not wait until we have sifted and weighed all our faults. In love, he begins where we are. Moved by this love, we have no need to savor past hurts caused by old enemies. Our ego has no need to nourish resentment, for it is supported, not by staying on top of personal relations, but by accepting forgiveness and freedom from God. We lose our masochistic taste for angry memories of the wrongs others have inflicted on us. We do not need to keep accurate score, for we do not need to be a moral winner. We forgive and start anew with what we now are and with what the other person now is.

Needless to say, agapic love does not shield us from hurt. Love is not a desensitizer. The loving person hurts, and he knows who and what caused the hurt. Love has the power to look cruel facts in the face, see them for what they are, even when aimed at us. Love does not blind us to reality or gloss over pain. But love's concern for the hurts of the one who causes hurt empowers us to forgive *before* we dig a channel for resentment in our memory.

The person who is driven by this love is in a position to be a servant of reconciliation in the world. Few people do have the power to throw away scorecards. Many more are driven to sad and sullen bitterness by their painful memories. Saddest of all is one who says: "I'll never forget what that man did to me." Not only is he tragic for his own sake, but his bitter memory keeps him from being a reconciler for others.

The person with the power to forget is the person who can bring others around to doing the same. Able to start fresh for himself, leaving past history's confusion tangled, he can carry on Christ's own ministry of reconciliation. He learns how to help people wipe from the record book all the old scores they have kept against each other. Love is that person's power. Love is the power that drives us toward the *other* who has done us wrong because it is able to tear up every moral scorecard. This is reconciliation, and reconciliation is love's ultimate goal.

9
Love Hates Evil

LOVE DOES NOT ENJOY EVIL. On the face of it, this seems a trivial virtue. What feeble praise for the power of divine love to observe that it does not rejoice in evil! Does not everyone with the minutest touch of decency *at least* hate evil? Why, then, is so minor a trait singled out as a bright excellence of divine love?

Could it be that we all really do rejoice in evil? Perhaps rejoicing in evil is in fact the norm, not the exception, and that *not* rejoicing in evil is so difficult for us that only the power of God's love can get us to hate evil? Anyone who is glad for evil would naturally be a little sneaky about it. We would obscure our seals of approval for it by semantic sleight of hand and probably not even admit it to ourselves in plain words.

We *do* rejoice in evil, even if we do not scream "Bravo!" at every mean and sordid sin. All it takes to rejoice in evil is to approve of its being here, to be content that we have some evil around, to endorse its presence in our world. We may even regret most of the evil in the world — especially that which hurts us — but we do rejoice in evil if we approve any of it at all.

It is not difficult to find reasons to be glad about evil. Sometimes our reasons are philosophical. Some of us even appeal to theology to help us approve of evil. But all of us at some time discover some reason for approval when evil strikes at other people's door. You may decide for yourself whether this sinister indictment is true of you. If it is, if even a subtle suggestion that evil is tolerable is allowed, it is in violent resistance to the power of love.

Before we get down to cases, we should arrive at a simple definition of evil. By evil, I mean everything that happens which hurts people needlessly. Now perhaps there are evils that do not hurt anyone, but if there are they are not the kind we shall be talking about. There are also things that hurt people necessarily — like dentists' drills and surgeon's knives; these we do not call evils since they are necessary to bring about something good. Of course, there will be some disagreement about which hurts are "necessary."

Sometimes evil is intentional; we call it moral evil. Sometimes evil is unintentional; we call this natural evil. Intentional evil is done by devils and people. Natural evil is done by nature, though devils and people sometimes cooperate. Somewhere in-between is accidental evil, the kind done by people when they do not mean to do it.

We shall think of anything that hurts people needlessly — whether done by nature or people or demons, whether done intentionally or accidentally — when we talk about evil that we rejoice in. Now let us examine whether love's power to resist rejoicing in evil is after all a power we need. We shall begin by noting a few common ways people do rejoice in evil.

There are subtle ways to rejoice in evil.

1. Philosophical rejoicing. Sometimes people rejoice in evil by way of a philosophical explanation of it. Profound thinkers are always tempted to locate a decent place for evil in our world. Orderly minds often cannot stand to see loose ends dangling about in the universe. They want all the pieces of the system to fit together. When their desire for order drives them to push everything back to one cause, they are monists. Certain that *everything* flows from a single ultimate source, they have to try to find a respectable place for evil along with everything else.

Monists tell us we can find a proper place for evil if we only try to see the big picture. Good and evil, they say, come together in our world like the black and white pieces of a mosaic. If you stand too close to it, all you see are scattered black and white stones. The presence of the two colors (standing for good and evil) makes no particular sense; in fact, they may seem to be random patches of conflicting colors. But if you step back far enough to see the entire scene, you recognize that each piece of stone belongs just where it is. All together, they make a splendid mosaic.

So it is, these orderly thinkers tell us, with good and evil in our world. If you are too close to it, you respond only to what hurts you or your family, or what you see on tonight's news. Life looks like a crazy, senseless, string of one evil after another, crashing into your world with painful assaults on your comfort. But if you can manage the really big picture in your thoughts, you will see that good and evil fit together in a grand mosaic — the universe of light and darkness. You will see that we need evil to complete the picture, just as Rembrandt needed shadow along with light to create his great paintings. Thus, you *can* rejoice in evil, because it contributes to what, finally, has to be a very good, if not the best possible world.

But love will not join this profound praise of evil. To be sure, love will put up with untidy worlds, and will stand far enough away to see the whole mosaic, but love sees evil only as a monstrous blot on God's creation. It sees a masterpiece vandalized. It is not seduced by profound speculations about universal harmony. When love sees evil, close by or from a philosophical mountaintop, it cries *"Foul!"* Evil, in love's eye, is obscene, no matter how splendidly and fully it is dressed.

2. Theological rejoicing. There is also a theological way of coming to terms with evil. It grows out of an unqualified belief that God is sovereign over human affairs and natural history. Nothing happens, whether in the infinite expanse of space or the nooks and crannies of our private lives, that God did not design or decree in eternity's conference room before time began.

But if God decrees it all, does he decree evil? Did he somehow *want* evil to get its ugly hands on his beautiful world? Did he *want* evil to distort and destroy human lives? Most of us who believe in the Lord of the universe choke on the very question. "No," we say, "he did not desire evil!" Some, however, stare this issue in the face and do not blink.

Look beyond the hurts of the moment, they say; take the long view of eternity. You will see that all evil will add to God's glory. Without evil, God would never have won a victory over evil. Without evil, God would never have been able to save a human soul from evil. God needed evil to bring out the best and noblest in him. We would never even have known how great God's love is had there been no evil for him to forgive. And we would never know his wrath were there no evildoers condemned in hell. Thus, evil enhances God. God is glorified by it.

Now I know of no Christian theology that actually advocates that we "rejoice in evil." No Christian hymnbook has ever included a doxology to evil. But the theology that insists God is praised by evil comes a single pulse-beat from leading us to be glad for evil.

Love will not move us a millimeter in the direction of affirming evil. It is the power standing in the way of yielding to the temptation to believe that God, in search of glory, gives evil a decent niche in his world. Living in love, we cannot be seduced by deep theology into a friendly view of evil. God is love. Love is the stark, uncompromised, absolute antithesis of evil. Evil, as we said, is any needless hurting of people; love is the power that moves only to heal needless hurts. Evil is a strange, mysterious power whose ultimate origin no one can fathom; love is simply and clearly of God. Love does not rejoice in evil, not even in the name of theological profundity.

3. Religious rejoicing. Religion may also rejoice in evil. We shall talk briefly about how religion approves of evil in its worship.

We worship whatever we think most worthy, but sometimes religion leads us to worship things that are unworthy of the soul's devotion. When religion builds altars to things less than God it brings out people's tendency to applaud evil. Idols always seduce us into an illicit affair with evil.

Take devotion to one's country, for example. Patriotism, love of one's nation, is how we express loyalty to the natural group which is second only to the family. But we can transform patriotism into a religious loyalty, making the state our supreme commitment. Once that happens, we are ripe for a perversion. For when we make anything an object of devotion, we stop criticizing it. We do not call our ultimates to account.

When we worship the created state above the creator God, we are ready to call evil good. We need only remember the ecstatic *"Sieg, Heil!"* chanted as a ritual Hosanna to Hitler to know that patriotism can become religion. And we need only remember how many of the worshipers consented to the monstrous evils of the divinized, demonized Nazi regime. But we need not look back or too far away. Patriotism slips over into idolatry in any land. American Christians must ask whether their terribly tardy recognition of the evil of the war in Vietnam was not grounded in a refusal to call their country's actions into critical doubt. Refusal to criticize was the flipside of idol worship. And this refusal moved us near to praise of evil.

Now and then religion's praise of evil takes off its disguise. It openly worships evil itself and the father of evil in cults of Satan worship. For the most part, this is a blasphemy of ecstasy. After flirtation with evil, shadowed by hesitation and plagued by guilt, a person is finally seduced into satanic intercourse. All devious game-playing is finished, he or she thinks. Now finally, it is possible not only to rejoice in evil but to rejoice in one's rejoicing. One has *dared* to say: "Evil, I love you." He or she is then a religious hero, for having dared the ultimate evil. I mention this only to observe that it happens. It probably is no more serious a threat to religion in general than the future of the family is threatened when an angry teen-ager screams, "Mother, I hate you."

4. Personal rejoicing. We also rejoice in evil in more direct and personal ways — sometimes when other people are hurt by evil, sometimes even when they do evil.

We rejoice when our enemies suffer evil. The more certain we are that our cause is right, the more pure our joy when the other side suffers. War provides the most grotesque instances of this. It is an axiom that the most righteous crusades became excuses for the worst evil. How many tears were shed in American homes during World War II when news came that Dresden, Germany, a city void of military significance, had been annihilated? How much anguish was spent when the first atom bomb fell on Hiroshima? Ironically, the more certain we are of our goodness, the more fitting it seems to rejoice in evil.

Our rejoicing when people do evil comes in cunning and subtle ways. Indeed, we may disguise our joys so that we ourselves will not recognize them — for fear of being shamed by them. We *rejoice* when we think we are only indignant, disgusted, or nauseated. Take the discovery that someone we know — but have never liked very well — has fallen into public sin. To make matters worse, this is a Christian leader, a prominent person in the church. Even more outrageous, the sin is a sexual sin. Some of us will rise to the occasion in full measure of indignant fury. Others will only be disgusted. The media will no doubt decide that this is "news fit to print." And so we will all have a chance to enjoy the evil.

We will let our moral energy work itself into a storm and relish the occasion to do so. We will enjoy our disgust so much that we would be furious were we to be deprived of it. While we say, "That sort of thing is sickening," we are probably savoring the bad taste as we mouth the words. Life without an occasional scandal would rob us of the joy of indignation and disgust. A well-ordered world must have some evil.

Even people large of soul rejoice in evil. A magnanimous spirit needs a little evil to exercise its talent. What is an empathetic soul to do if it cannot now and then stretch out an arm to embrace a fallen brother or sister? It makes such a person feel good to be forgiving and compassionate. He rejoices in evil because every evil gives him a new chance to be a *notably* large-souled person.

In these cleverly disguised ways we rejoice in evil suffered and in evil done. We are selective, to be sure. We never rejoice when children die of malnutrition in Bangladesh. We do not rejoice when our husband has a coronary. Whether far away on a grand scale or close by in small doses, most evil that strikes people down does not give us joy. But when it hurts just a little we may be tempted to rejoice.

If you are a mediocre student, struggling to stay afloat in competitive graduate classes, it is tempting to rejoice if others in your class receive C's when you managed a B. If your business turns sour and your creditors are knocking at the door, while your friends are all doing splendidly, it is tempting to rejoice on the day their stocks take a sudden tumble. If you are competing for a job, and someone applies who seems more qualified than you are, but at the last moment betrays a weakness that costs him the job, you are tempted to rejoice in the evil that he suffers. If your children are rebelling, while the children of your friends are making their parents proud, the news that your friend's successful child has gotten into trouble makes you feel good, though you know your friend is suffering.

We do rejoice in evil, all too easily. Other people's sins make us look virtuous. We need an occasional scandal to inflate our meager virtue. Other people's misfortunes make our lot easier to bear. We need people around us — friends and enemies alike — who suffer now and then to give our bad luck some company.

Love rejects evil.

Love, in contrast, is a power that moves us only to regret evil — anywhere, in any form, by any cause. Love drives us toward others with no expectation of reward, not even that of illicit smidgens of delight from the evil they suffer. This is a paradox, for agapic love, like God, does its best work in response to evil. In a sense it is true that evil makes agape real. It builds a stage on which love is forgiving, healing, and redeeming. But love rejoices only when evil is destroyed. In some delicate sense, then, pure agapic love would be glad to be needed no more.

Love has eyes only for those struck by evil; it is driven only to heal. The person set free by love can never rejoice in the evil that makes love necessary. What he knows of evil is only that it needlessly hurts and destroys. Righteous indignation may rejoice in evil. The person who "takes offense" at evil may relish the chance to be offended. But the person moved by love has eyes only for the wounds in the body or soul of a person; so he cannot rejoice in the evil that caused them.

While love does not rejoice in evil, the song goes on, it does rejoice "with the truth." Why is it truth, not goodness, that is contrasted with evil? Why not the obvious conflict: love does not rejoice in evil, but rejoices in goodness? Then, too, why does Paul say *"with* the truth" instead of the more natural *"in* the truth" (which is how some English versions translate it)? Our task, of course, is not to wonder why St. Paul did not say what we expect him to, but to make sense of what he meant by what he did say.

Take the word "with" first. Truth is love's favorite consort. Love is at its best with truth at its side. Love *needs* the truth, or it turns into fuzzy-headed pathos. Without a good grip on truth — that is, on reality — love floats like dreaming desire through a fog of maudlin wishes.

Truth keeps love honest, reminding it that an enemy loved is still an enemy, a sinner forgiven no less a sinner. Truth keeps love from sweeping the realities about people under a shaggy carpet of agapic good will. So love rejoices *with* the truth.

But love also returns the favor, for love keeps truth honest. Without love, truth's obsession with facts distorts those facts. A sheer fact, about evil for instance, soon becomes a false-hood. A sheer fact, shorn of personal relationships, turns quickly into a lie. It may be a fact that someone you know has committed a sensational sin. But love knows the difference between falling into sin and programming it into one's life. The sheer fact that a person has done a single evil can blind us to a redeeming lifetime. Love rejoices *with* the truth because love widens the scope of truth's lenses to include the whole person.

Now we must ask why the song pits truth (instead of goodness) against evil. The answer is found in the Bible's notion of what truth is.

We can say three things about what the Bible means by truth. First, truth is larger than accurate statements, correct figures, and consistent reasoning. Second, truth refers to reality: things are true when they are right, what they ought to be and where they ought to be in relation to each other. Truth is reality when it matches God's purpose. Third, truth is a person, a person whose acts and words blend to draw a profile of human life as God meant it to be lived. In this way, Jesus could say: "I *am* the truth." When one meets Jesus as truth, he learns what God has in mind for human life, what reality is meant to be on earth.

Now we can listen to the line again and feel the rhythm of its meaning: "Love does not rejoice in evil, but rejoices with the *truth*." Love rejoices with the truth which is Jesus Christ, and rejoicing with Christ we revel in reality as it is meant to be. We are glad to be alive in a world where truth can be known uniquely as the reality that is Jesus Christ. Evil is anything that hurts people needlessly. Christ came to save people from evil, so rejoicing in evil and rejoicing with truth are *absolute* antitheses.

Rejoicing with the truth puts us on the side of the future. For we are not faced merely with a choice between two great cosmic antagonists. We are faced with a choice between the winner and the loser. To rejoice with the truth is to bet your life on Christ as victor over evil.

God's love, once experienced, opens our eyes to the real state of affairs in our universe. In the first place, love lets us see that evil never *belongs* anywhere; it has no right to exist. There is only one thing to do with it. Crush it, destroy it. Love drives us to will *only* good for persons and thus forces us to see anything that hurts them needlessly as an intolerable evil.

In the second place, love opens our minds to the possibility that evil has in fact been defeated. Love opens us to the truth of Jesus Christ, who met evil head-on. At no other time in history was a person hurt so badly. But he, in love, absorbed the full shock and came back to win. The truth is victory over evil; this *is* reality. No wonder that love rejoices with the truth.

Love, then, will not give evil a decent spot in God's world; love will not let us sneak evil into a grand and good scheme. Evil cannot gain respectability in the presence of love. What love knows about evil is that, in all its horrible and mysterious forms, it is doomed by Jesus Christ to lose even the leech's hold it has on life now. Beyond that, love leaves evil shrouded in ultimate mystery.

There is more that love does not tell us. It does not give us the inside story of how God, who wills only our good, is involved with pain. Love knows that God never inflicts pain needlessly, and that pain might be God's chosen route to blessing for us. But it does not predict how pain, seen from a later time, might appear as a necessary link with joy. Not all pain is evil. It may be that love, in some wonderful turn of events, may rejoice in past pain. But it rejoices in pain only when it discerns that pain was a necessary instrument of greater blessing.

Even where evil is just plain evil, good may come *in* it. Love well knows that God is able to bring blessing out of evil. But it is one thing to say that good was brought out of evil; it is quite another to call evil good on that account. Nothing is more important to keep clear than this.

A little five-year-old girl is playing near the curb in front of her house. A drunk driver happens by, loses control of his car, and strikes her dead. Her parents choke on the bitterness of needless evil. They look to each other, look to heaven, cry to God. They know in their hearts that there is nothing here but evil. No soothing words from decent-minded friends will soften the terrible truth of the evil of this event.

Yet, as father and mother grope their way through the tunnel of horror with no light at the end, they rediscover each other in the darkness of their night. God is silent. Friends are powerless. Yet, as their souls throb in pointless pain, they move awkwardly into the only truth there is in the whole world for them: *we have a future together*. Putting a hand in the hand of the other, each comes to know that, in spite of hell in their private world, life is worth trying to live. As this almost unbelievable truth begins to grip their souls, they find — maybe for the first time — that they came to life's paramount discovery *together*. Revelation has happened; light has dawned; inspiration has seized them. They know together that life is good in spite of everything. And, on looking back, they know it was of God.

As the days of ordinary life overtake them, they look back in painful thought. Each parent looks back on the days of their evil with ambivalent feelings. Nothing so good ever had come to their lives together. Never before had a look into each other's eyes revealed so much understanding of each other's heart. Never had they felt so strong as in the hour of their utter weakness. Never had the power to affirm life felt so tender and beautiful. The days of mourning were the best days of their life together.

Still, their love never can *rejoice* in that evil. No philosopher could seriously suggest to them that it was a good thing for that man to have driven when he was drunk and killed their precious child. No theologian's logical sleight of hand could persuade them that the fatal assault on their little one was somehow a minor episode in the great unraveling of eternal destiny, and that therefore it was really good. No pastor, innocently seizing on God's ability to reveal himself within the circle of evil, could persuade them to call their evil a good. The good that was experienced within evil did not make the evil a good. The parents would trade back all the discovered good for the return of their daughter. What happened was an evil. Love will never rejoice in it. Love will only rejoice in the good that came in spite of it.

Realism is the secret of love's patience. Love is not idealism; it does not have to be fanatic. It is not hysterical; it knows the world is not going to fall apart unless we immediately clean up every mess. Love's patience is no mushy fantasy that people are all really very nice. Love knows that we live in a mixture of good and evil. Love knows that life now is ambiguous. But love can bear it. Love can even rejoice in this mixed-up life because it rejoices with the truth, the Truth who will "reconcile all things to himself" (Colossians 1:20) and thus make the whole world *true* again. Love manages well in a world like ours; but love never approves of the evil that makes our good world the mixed reality it is.

10
Love Bears All Things

LOVE BEARS ALL THINGS. Reading this simple line, we touch the hem of some deep cosmic secret. Love sustains and supports all things. Everything rests on the power of love. My personal consciousness of myself is rooted in love, and the vitality of civilizations flows from the secret power of love. Love carries all things. This is love's large arena of power. But the line of our song has less cosmic possibilities as well.

Behind the English word in our simple sentence lies the Greek verb *stego*, translated as "bear." *Stego* has several meanings, depending on its associations. It could mean here that love *bears up* under all things, that love has the power to endure a lot. St. Paul uses *stego* this way in 1 Thessalonians 3:5. But our song expresses this very thought three lines later. It is thus more likely that Paul's thought here is not that love bears up under things, but that it bears all things *up*. We shall assume here that the meaning is: Love *carries* everything. But before we discuss *how* love really can carry things, there is another translation of *stego* that we must hear; it is too provocative to pass unnoticed.

Love covers things up.

"Love covers a multitude of sins " (1 Peter 4:8). *Stego* is the Greek verb for covering up. Love keeps us quiet, tempering our tendency to say too much too quickly. Love has a fine sense for when to keep its mouth shut.

Love hates a scandal. Scandals are scurrilous, always indecent. But love drives us away from scandal for deeper reasons than propriety and good taste. Scandal hurts people; and love hates everything that hurts people needlessly. This is why a loving person is turned off by gossip and rumor — out of concern for the people being whispered about. Love is hurt, too, by exposés of the sensational sins of famous people. Love will not put out a cent for yellow journalism. It will not agree that the media have the calling to tell us everything. The old *New York Times* motto, "All the News That's Fit to Print," implied that some things were not fit — even if they were factual. Love is in tune with this position.

Love covers up for the sake of healing. It keeps things quiet so that persons can be healed behind the scenes. Jesus himself taught us this when he told us how to respond when a brother or sister has done you wrong. Keep it between the two of you, if possible; and if that does not work, keep it within a small circle. Let the church know only as a last resort (Matthew 18:15). This is love's cover-up, love's way of keeping space and time for healing.

There is a limit. Love covers a multitude of sins, but not *all*. There are some hidden evils that cannot be undone unless they are publicized. To undo evils that hurt people love drives us to expose them. Where there is covert torture of political prisoners, love drives us to lift the cover that shields the evil. Where political leaders betray their trust, their betrayal must be made public. Wherever secret evil in centers of power inflicts injustice on people, love will drive us to ferret it out. Love exposes for the same reason it covers — the good of persons.

Love covers up and love exposes. Wisdom is the power to tell us *when* to do which. Love seeks justice while it seeks healing of persons. If public exposure of guilty persons will reduce the chances of healing, love covers up for them. But when secrecy threatens justice, love lifts the cover. In any given situation, the sensitivity of love must go hand-in-hand with the discernment of wisdom to tell us what to do.

Love carries personal burdens.

Let us now attend to the meaning that comes to mind first: "Love carries all things." This fits what we already know about love: it holds things up, supports them, carries them along. These are the daily works of love. Carrying things is love's full-time job.

Love carries people's burdens. When we hear that love carries all things, we think first of its power to support the burden-bearers of the world. Why is love a burden-carrier? Why should it drive us to bear burdens for neighbors? The answer is that love drives us to do things for people that they cannot do for themselves. No one can carry every burden alone — or indeed almost any burden alone. To carry it alone presses our very humanity from us. We are created to be *with* somebody in our burden bearing. We go against the grain of our personhood when we try to be strong, silent, secret sustainers of our own burdens. If we bear everything alone, our souls shrink.

But is there not something noble about accepting our own burden instead of dumping it on others? Do most of us not really prefer people who keep their troubles to themselves? And does the Bible itself not suggest that each of us should be responsible for his own burdens (Galatians 6:5)? Surely there is a point here that might restrain over eager burden-sharers. Love is not an open invitation for everyone to dump burdens on soft-headed Christian lovers. We are not compelled by love always to pick up everybody's check. Nor is your love an excuse for me to dump all my private problems on you so that you can get spiritual credit for loving. Your love is not my escape from my burdens. But I am equally wrong to insist on bearing them alone, for I cannot.

Knowing people, God realized that we could not manage our burdens alone. Being love, he was moved to carry them with us. "Surely he has borne our griefs and carried our sorrows" (Isaiah 53:4). God joined us on earth as a burden-carrier, even to the extent of carrying the burden of being in the wrong: "he bore the sin of many" (Isaiah 53:12). God became a burden-bearer *with* us. But he did not relieve us of responsibility for our burdens. Though he bore our griefs, we still have griefs to carry. He carried our guilt, but we still have guilt to bear. The cross was not an end to human sorrow, nor Jesus' death the death of human guilt. How, then, does God's love really bear our burden?

Consider the burden of guilt. God's love does not take away our guilt. Guilt is a reality about ourselves that nothing can erase. One secret of living in God's love, however, is having the courage to accept guilt. We stop our whimpering excuses and silly evasions, own up to guilt, and then accept forgiveness. Love's sacrifice carried away judgment. Christ bore our condemnation. The art of living with God now is the art of accepting guilt without accepting judgment and condemnation for it. It is an art that anyone can learn once opened to the love that moved Christ to bear guilt *with* us and judgment *for* us.

Love carries some things away.

Divine love also carries our sorrows. Sorrow is a suffering of the mind, the hurt of knowing that something is wrong. We are sorry when we are conscious of our own suffering or of the suffering of people we care about. To sorrow is to feel spiritual distress, loss, guilt, and pain. God's love moved him to become, with us, a "man of sorrows" (Isaiah 53:3).

Does love carry our sorrows *away* from us? Can anyone love us enough to diminish our burden and reduce our sorrow? Can we love another person in a way that takes away sorrow from his soul? How could love do this miracle?

Consider, first, that sorrow and suffering are not measured in quantity. They are not divisible. If I suffer along with you, I cannot take away one-half of your suffering. If two people in a room have a hangover, there is a lot of pain in the room, but if eight more people joined them with throbbing heads of pain, we would not have five times as much pain in the room as before. When a thousand mothers cry because their children go to bed hungry, there is no more sorrow in a thousand breasts than in any single mother's heart.

We do not multiply sorrow and suffering as we do dollars, nor can we divide it among people. There is a way — as we shall see — of letting another person reduce our suffering by helping us bear it; but it is not by way of some mathematical redistribution of the burden.

We can suffer with another person in many ways. One way is actually to feel physical pain along with someone we love. Another is to feel sorrow for his or her pain. In sorrow, we share the consciousness of suffering. God entered our life to share our sorrow and suffering. He was hurt himself, and he sorrowed to the core of his heart at the wrongs and pain suffered by others. The Lord God became a burden-carrier with us. What hurt us are the burdens that hurt him. He carried our burden, though he does not take it away.

Sometimes people suffer the same acute physical pain they know a loved one is undergoing. There is no physiological explanation for this; the only cause is love. I have heard of cases in which a person suffered the same pains as a loved one though not even aware of the loved one's suffering. Such events illustrate how little we really know about love's power to share pain. More familiar is sympathy — love's power to share sorrow, to join with another person in the mental or spiritual pain of being conscious of loss or hurt. In such cases we are able to enter someone's spiritual pain.

God came into human life as a man who shared our pain and sorrow. We remember how the Man of Sorrows was hurt with the horrible pain of crucifixion, but might he not have suffered the very physical pain of countless people besides? Who can say for certain what were the limits of the Lord's pain? In any case, he suffered doubly, for with his pain he also suffered an exquisite *consciousness* of all our pains and losses, and the consciousness was that of an infinite agapic love. In this way, he carried our sorrows with us, though he did not carry them all away.

The premise remains, of course, that this same Lord who carried our sorrows with us — and continues to carry them with us even now — will indeed some day take them away. In the vision of Revelation 21, the cure for sorrow is the presence of God-with-us: "he will wipe away every tear from their eyes." If he shares our sorrow, if he feels what we feel, he must be doubly determined to put an end to it. And if we know this about God, we know that his light shines beyond our darkness, and this makes our sorrow easier to bear now. In some sense, then, love does carry our sorrows away because it carries them *with* us.

Now let us look more closely at human sharing. Can human beings carry each other's burdens away? Can we diminish sorrow by sharing sorrow? God's love in us is the power to pierce the privacy of another's suffering and to feel the pain of it. If our neighbor carries the terrible grief of a lost child, our love feels the grief. If our neighbor overseas carries the burden of hunger, love moves us to suffer the burden with him. If a friend falls into sin, love moves us to carry even the guilt along with him. If we are not moved to carry our neighbor's burden we do not have love.

Does love carry people's burdens *away?* This question still needs to be answered. Can I reduce a neighbor's burden by taking it on myself? The answer is that loving entrance into the pain of another *can* carry pain away. The experience of pain is a deep mystery. We hardly know what pain is, though we have no doubts when we have it. Some of our pain is precisely that of having no burden-carrier in our lives. Consequently, some of the most dramatic relief comes when someone enters our lives and accepts our burdens as his. When persons truly share in their spirit a consciousness of our hurt or loss, and thus carry our sorrow, they carry some of it away from us. When love drives a person to share another's pain, the pain becomes less hard to bear. We say this in awe; for it touches one of the deepest mysteries of life.

Agapic love reduces suffering in a more obvious way. Persons in whom God lives are enabled by love to act for healing. To experience the love of a burden-bearing God is to be moved to heal the causes of sorrow, disease, and death. Love builds a leprosarium; love drives people to share their wealth with the hungry of the world; love drives the comfortable to participate in liberation of oppressed people. Love heals on a personal level. Love drives toward healing on a political level.

Love carries civilization — and the universe.

We have been speaking of love as the power to carry the burdens of others. Now let us turn this thought of love bearing all things into a very different direction and see love as that which carries *everything* that is good. Love holds all things together, carries them along, keeps them moving, sustains them. Love is the amazing power that makes the world go around and human history move ahead. Love is the power that sustains the universe itself; it is the invisible foundation for all the structures of life.

Love keeps the tattered edges of human culture from unraveling completely. It keeps the shaken foundational structures of civilization from crumbling. Love gives human society a future. Society exists when people are free participants in the wealth and responsibilities of the common life. Isolated from community, human existence is lonely, desperate, and brutish. Apart from society we have no personal identity; apart from love we have no society.

Unless society is knit together with love there is only efficient organization; and when efficiency is the highest value, persons are transformed into things whose value is their contribution to making things run. Without agapic love, efficiency can excuse anything; the weak, the voiceless, the unborn may all be sacrificed at the altar of efficiency. The Nazi state is the horrible corpse of a human society that died because people gave up on love for the sake of efficiency.

Laws will not sustain a society, even though without law a society is lost. Laws need love. Love provides insight into people; it recognizes genuine differences between them — their needs and their circumstances. So love helps law to be fair and flexible — to be the arm of humane justice.

Justice cannot sustain a society alone either. Nothing is enough without justice. But justice alone is not enough. Without love justice is brittle, callous, and legalistic, and eventually becomes unjust. Without love, justice is measured only by the letter of existing law. With love, justice responds to the real needs of real people, being flexible in response to unusual cases and special situations. Love keeps alive a holistic *vision* of a society where the weak, the poor, the oppressed, and all others who lack the power to press for justice will be full partners in the freedom and joy of the kingdom of God.

Finally, power alone cannot sustain a society. To be sure, society needs the ability to defend its interests and protect its preserves in our sinful world. But if society had only power, it would soon be a prison camp instead of a human society. Without love, power is only used as the threat of force. With love, power can be deployed on behalf of creative and compassionate justice. Love keeps power humane.

Society is held together by justice, laws, and power, but it is kept going as a truly human society only where love is the basic humanizing energy. Love keeps law and justice and power in balance. In a sinful world, that balance will always be precarious. Things are always going wrong. Yet, where love is powerful, it keeps them from going so badly wrong that chaos or tyranny will ultimately destroy society. Love carries society and keeps it human.

Love carries smaller groups within a society as well. For instance, love carries a marriage. Eros creates a marriage, driving two people together in a personal and sexual union. Eros gives marriage its peaks of mystery and adventure. But it also fans the flames of dispute and confrontation. And through the valleys of marital disappointment, anger, and pain, it is agape that carries the marriage.

Agape is the power for sticking with a marriage when the passion has burned down to dreary toleration. It is the power to wait and see if desire might be ignited, and eros re-created later. Agape is the energy to do the works of eros even when the feelings of eros are gone.

With agapic love what might otherwise be the causes of divorce can become the challenge of re-creation. Agape forgives the guilty spouse, affirms the unlovely spouse, bears with bad taste, insensitive neglect, stupid decisions, and cruel aggressiveness. With agape, two people can bear tough confrontation and mutual criticism and rise ready for healing from even the bitterest experience of anger and hate. Agape cannot create a marriage, but it can carry a marriage when eros is cold.

Finally, we may stretch our imagination to the point of taking our song literally: love carries the whole universe. Why did God create the cosmos? Moved by his own love's need he created that which he could love with pleasure. Why did the Creator stay with his creatures after they spurned his love? Moved by the loved one's need, he stayed with the earth until the time came for him to redeem it. Why did he stay with his piteous planet lurching down the tragic passages of sinful history? Given its metaphysical fragility and moral insanity, what keeps the universe going? The answer: agapic love carries the cosmos along.

Love carries *all* things. God's love is too grand to be confined as a feeling within my soul. The design of God's love is large indeed. No nook or cranny of history is too small for its concern; no civilization too large for its power. In Christ, we are part of a movement of love that rolls on through time toward a new earth where all things will be right, where we all will be vitalized wholly by the love of God. Meanwhile, love carries the world along, "not wishing that any should perish, but that all should reach repentance" (2 Peter 3:9) and share in the experience of total healing, the time of the new creation (2 Corinthians 5:17).

11
Love Believes All Things

WHEN IT COMES TO believing, there are three styles of people. On one side is the gullible person, who believes almost everything. What such a person believes depends on who gets to him first — or, perhaps, on who gets to him last. He believes television commercials, and sends money for every new gadget advertised during the breaks in the movies. He believes the gossip of the sensational newspapers he buys at the supermarket. He is sure that every used car salesman is sincere. He believes in flying saucers and believes the military conspires to keep the truth about them from us. The gullible person is ready to believe "all things."

At the other extreme is the cynic, who believes almost nothing. He calls himself a realist, and begins with the assumption that everyone is trying to get something from him. The cynic looks at everyone with cold distrust. People are never his neighbors, only competitors. Politicians are only lying opportunists. Preachers are in religion only for profit. Newspapers are parties to mass deception to protect the powerful. The cynic is disposed to believe only one thing: nobody is worth believing.

Somewhere between the gullible person and the cynic is the wise critic. He deals with people carefully, not assuming that all people are liars, but knowing well that some are. He suspects that most people will lie if necessary to protect their interests. He is willing to give anyone the benefit of the doubt for a time, but he is not willing to erase his doubts. He lets everyone prove his right to be believed. He trusts people, to a point. He does not believe all things, but he is prepared to believe if he has evidence that the other person is believable.

Love is careless.

Love believes all things. This line in our song seems to put love on the side of the gullible. Gullible people are not necessarily lovers, of course. People may be gullible because they are stupid or innocent or afraid to disbelieve. Gullibility is not a sign of love, but love, it seems, tends to make people gullible. We must look at this carefully.

Love is the opposite of cynicism. As we have said, love views the people around us as neighbors, not mere competitors, and love knows that neighbors are always people with needs. Hence, love transcends the basic cause for the cynic's chronic suspicions. But love does not quite follow the line of the careful critic either. The critic is too calculating for love, too reserved, too prudent, always on guard. Love relaxes its guard.

There is a careless streak in love. It can be careless with goods, pouring expensive perfume on a Master's feet and hair (John 12:3). A careful person would have measured it out beforehand — not too much (keeping some for oneself), not too little (ensuring that impression of generosity is given). Love is also careless with one's self. It is risky to put oneself out for another, to go out of one's way to help another person — when one is not sure of how to do it well. One may be misunderstood, deceived, hurt. We could flub our overtures of love and end up looking ridiculous. Moved by love, however, we overpower our fear and take the risk.

Love is careless, too, with trust. Love is ready to believe. Love can throw off reserve. It does not worry too much about being cheated, because it has eyes only for the other's needs. If love seems a little naive it is not for lack of experience with people, but because love does not bother to calculate the odds on people. Love just zeroes in on them as sinful, weak, needy persons. No wonder people must sometimes be rescued from their own love.

Love and faith together lead to belief.

We should take careful stock of love's role in Christian belief. St. Paul is not laying on us a duty to believe everything. He is singing of the impulse of love. Love is a believing power, an impulse that moves us to trust people. It may be that on some occasions wisdom will tell us to hold back love's impulse toward belief. But the fact remains that love is one impulse that pushes us toward belief.

It is also true that faith is the impulse of love. It was James who said that faith must move us to love. Had he been writing poetically in chapter 2:14-17, James might have said that "faith loves all things." That is, *true* faith is the power of love.

It works both ways. Faith loves and love believes. The two are never separable from each other. At the center of a person's Christian experience we cannot really tell the difference between faith and love. At the core one's faith is an open heart to the love of God in Christ Jesus. John Calvin said that faith is nothing at all but the heart's "open container," ready to receive the love that God gives through Jesus Christ. So faith is openness to love, readiness to receive love. Faith is the *experience* of being loved. And from this experience of God's love comes a readiness to believe the *truths* of the Christian gospel.

How, then, does love make believers of us?

We have already answered this question in terms of Christian belief. The deepest motive for believing is the awareness of being loved by God. What first brings a person to faith is a sense that God has grasped one at the depths of life, reaching out somehow from the cross of Christ to secure one in love. Feeling this, one lays down disbelief and becomes a believer. What keeps that person believing is the experience of being held, controlled, subdued, and surrounded by God's love. In the long run, one keeps believing because one cannot escape the love of God. Hence, we can say that faith is first of all the experience of being loved by God. Then faith leads us on to belief of truths about God, especially about his love.

Love is the deepest of many reasons for believing.

There are many other reasons people believe; none but love is the deep and real reason.

Some of us believe because a tradition of faith and love permeated the homes in which we grew up. We believe because we were reared in belief. A reporter once asked the great theologian Karl Barth, "Sir, you've written many great volumes about God, but how do you know it is true?" Barth thought only a moment and said: "Because my mother told me so." Likewise, many believers could revise the children's song to read: "Jesus loves me, this I know, for *my mother* told me so." Believing families are the means God uses to keep faith alive. But the fact is that some children *stop* believing because of parents who had strong beliefs and little love. Parental guidance is not the deepest reason for belief.

All of us believe because of the church. Protestants may feel uneasy with St. Augustine's words: "I would not have believed had it not been for the church." Not all of us are ready to concede the church this much influence in our faith life. But Augustine was really speaking for all who believe. The church is God's medium for keeping the message alive through the ages. The medium is not the message, but the message of love would have been long lost without the medium. The Word of God has been passed down to us through the church. The sacrament of Christ's death celebrated there has channeled his grace to us.

The church, the clumsy body in which Christ has walked the streets of the world, is one reason for believing. Yet for all that faith owes to the church, the church has also been the cause of considerable unbelief in the world. The church is a reason for some people to refuse to believe. It is a chosen instrument, but not the deepest source of faith.

Some people may believe because of the evidence supported by convincing arguments for faith. There *are* arguments for believing. There are arguments to prove that God exists. There are arguments to prove that Jesus rose from the dead. Some of the arguments are weak; some strong, perhaps persuasive. There are effective arguments to show at least that it is not stupid or irrational to believe. Such arguments, by helping us see that belief can make sense, support us in our believing. But, for every persuasive argument *for* believing, an argument against believing is waiting in the wings for someone smart enough to see it. Logic may convince believers that their belief is intellectually respectable but it cannot be the deepest reason for believing.

Some people are sure they believe because they know the Bible is true. First they are persuaded that the Bible is true, and so they believe what it tells us about Jesus Christ and God's love. This may be some people's experience. But it is not most people's experience. Most people come to trust the Bible because through it they have met God in Jesus Christ. Trusting the book is a consequence of trusting the person, not the other way around.

No, the power for belief is love. The other vehicles are only *means*. The power for belief is the love we discover when God first encounters us. Love shatters our reasons for disbelief. Love disarms our hearts and captures our minds and sets us free from the prisons of our own ego-driven lives. It grasps us at the center of life and will not let go. In the words of Francis Thompson's great poem "The Hound of Heaven," love pursues us with "deliberate speed, majestic instancy" while we are in flight from it. It catches and defeats us in our prideful resistance to love and gives us power to receive God's own love to us. This is the belief-creating power of love.

We have been saying that love is the power for believing the truth of the gospel, but is it also a power that drives us to believe each other? Does love believe all things about people?

Love does not literally believe *everything*. As we have said, Paul is singing, and his poetic impulse happily prevails over literal precision. There are definite things love does not believe — like tawdry gossip. Love may go beyond common sense; it does not subscribe to nonsense. Love is ready to believe all that *ought* to be believed.

Agape, however, moves us to believe in people, because it is secure love. It is not in competition for power, money, applause, even for love. So it is not on edge; it is not anxious. It never has anything to lose. It does not fear being taken advantage of, made a fool of, or being let down.

Agape has nothing to lose. It is in the business of giving itself away. How could it be deceived; how could it be betrayed? It is invulnerable. For its strength is inexhaustible; its very power is in its giving. And out of this strength, it is prepared to believe.

Love moves us, for instance, to believe that every person is of great worth. The hard evidence of behavior may count against this belief. A person's record may suggest a cogent line of argument to the effect that his death would improve the world. Yet love believes. Love believes that the incorrigible liar is of supreme value, that the most corrupt dictator has a redeemable soul, that every killer on Death Row is a person of irreducible worth.

Love does not turn its head away from facts. Love looks the ugly, cruel facts straight in the face. Love looks at the liar and calls him a liar. Love looks at the sadistic dictator and calls him evil. Love does not excuse the rapist, the looter, or the corrupt politician. Love just sees more than the honest eye can see. Love sees the person beneath the facts, the hardest facts, about him. And love *believes* that that person is of inestimable worth, is redeemable, and can become good.

Often, love goes against the grain of our desires. There are some people whom we dislike too much to want to see redeemed. There are public figures whom we long to see put down and eliminated. There are people so obnoxious, on our view, that we cannot believe that they *deserve* to be saved. We feel this way because we do not love them. In the power of love, we believe all things, even that a wretched person is a real and, therefore, a redeemable person.

Love, in short, is the power to believe more than the evidence requires. Profligate in its belief, uncritical in its trust, love can get us into trouble if we calculate costs. It can use our own money and time and energy and deprive us of ego-pleasure. But in terms of what we *really* are, persons whom God loves *unconditionally*, we cannot lose by love's trust. We know that we are what we are because God has seen beneath the layers of dubious quality and ordinary sin and discerned in us persons worth redeeming. So, when our love is betrayed, we have really lost nothing at all. What could we lose that is most deeply ours when all that we have is the product of God's love? One who is much loved owes much. One who loves much believes much.

We cannot live by Christian love alone. We also live by wisdom and intelligence. We are moved by justice. We are driven by eros. All of these will put checks and balances on love's readiness to believe. In our world love needs such balances. But in the long run we are far better off trusting people too much than trusting too little. Being taken in now and then is a small price to pay — if it has to be paid — for not letting a neighbor down. Besides, trusting people is training for trusting God.

12
Love Hopes
All Things

LOVE IS THE POWER of hope. As long as a person loves, he is able to hope. The power of love overcomes the drift to despair, and prevails against every urge to resign. It resists the demonic drive toward despondency. Love keeps us hopeful, in all situations, against all evidence. "Love hopes all things."

On the human level hope keeps love alive. As we have seen, erotic love is born of need and grows with desire. At some moment need and desire fix on a specific person, and love is born. But romantic love needs a hope that the other person will become a lover in return.

When such hope is lost, love eventually goes with it. An alcoholic husband who has turned his wife's everyday life into a hellish nightmare strains hope. As the wife's hope for any change dies, her love gradually turns into a grim struggle for survival. Loss of hope has meant loss of love. Sooner or later a parent whose son rebels against and finally rejects all the values of the home faces a challenge of both love and hope. Love is still felt in the form of heartache, but it stays only as long as the parent hopes for change. As years go by and the rejection becomes increasingly implacable, that hope begins to die; and the parent, often fearfully and shamefully, feels a slow death of love.

Sometimes we are not sure whether we are still loving or only trying to love. We become unsure of our love as we lose hope that it will bear fruit. How long can we love without the hope that our love will be returned? How long can we love an enemy without the hope of his one day becoming a friend? How long can we love a spouse if our estrangement is so deep that we lose hope of reunion? One thing is clear: human love needs at least the glimmer of hope for love returned.

What is hope?

We have seen that human love needs human hope. Now we need to see also that human hope needs divine love. Let us begin by looking a little more closely at what sort of thing hope is.

Hope is first of all a desire. The desire in hope is more than a wish; it is strong enough for us to *will* it. We often wish for things that we do not really desire; in our fantasies we have the luxury of wishing for things we would not really want to complicate our lives with. There are some things we may wish for but not really want because we know that having them would prevent us from having something we want more. A man may wish to have a mistress, but he may not will to have one because he wants his marriage more. A woman may wish for freedom from the demands of her four children; she may wish to be single again, unencumbered, pursuing a reward-ing profession untrammeled by family responsibilities. But her love for her husband and the happiness of her life as mother may keep her from willing what she wishes. Dreams are often made of wishes we do not really want, but hope is a desire for something that we *will* to have.

In hope expectancy is added to desire. The expectancy of hope is more than a sense of what things are likely to happen, for some things that we think are likely to happen frighten us and we do not will that they happen at all. When we hope, we expect that what we *want* to happen is really going to happen. To be hopeful is to face the future with some gladness, some thankfulness, some sense that the present is worth living because we expect the future to bring what we deeply desire.

For Paul, however, hope has an added dimension beyond desire and even expectancy. Hope is *certainty*. He speaks of "a hope [that] does not disappoint us" (Romans 5:5). This idea differs radically from the way we often use the word "hope." In daily human experience, we fall back on something we call hope precisely when we lose our confidence: by hope we mean a lapse into desire *without* expectancy. When at wit's end we say, "All we can do now is hope," we are not talking Christian hope.

The promise of Christ is that *he* is our hope. This hope cannot fail because Christ will not and cannot fail. This is why Christian hope is often symbolized by an anchor, "a sure and steadfast anchor of the soul" (Hebrews 6:19). Hope in Christian experience means: "I am *sure* as I face the future." Now we should note that this is true "because God's love has been poured into our hearts through the Holy Spirit" (Romans 5:5). Love is the power behind the hope that "does not disappoint us." Love stimulates the certainty of Christian hope.

Are we playing games, indulging in pious fantasies? Does love create confidence that a miracle is always on the way? Does love give us power to "know" that our mother's cancer will be cured? Does love tell parents that their son's leukemia will go away? Does love assure every estranged spouse that his or her marriage will be healed? The answer to questions like this is No. Love cannot make us certain about everything. Love's hopes in fact often disappoint us. How, then, can we sing "Love hopes all things" within a reality where hopes are too often smashed by brute facts?

Hope at its deepest is not focused on particulars. At its core hope looks *beyond* a cure for disease, a solution for a problem, an escape from pain, for assurance from God that life has point and meaning in spite of disease, problems, and pain. Hope looks to the promise of the final victory of Jesus Christ over all that hurts and kills. This is the hope that gives a person courage to praise today and to face tomorrow with expectancy even when one does not expect the problem to be solved. Love breeds this hope in both the person loved and the loving person.

Love gives hope to the person loved.

Love gives hope to the person who is loved. Such hope can be inspired by a sense of being cared for, even in situations where science offers little hope. In Duarte, California, there is a hospital dedicated to what are often called catastrophic illnesses, called "The City of Hope." Two members of my immediate family have been patients in this hopeful hospital, and I know from experience how hope can be aroused in a caring institution. There are patients here with terminal diseases, but there are no "hopeless cases." The reason there are no "hopeless cases" is that there are no *cases* at all, only persons. The hospital philosophy holds that a sick body is a person and a person is a whole person only within the context of his family. Every member of the staff is called on to relate to patients as persons in their total setting. They are to be treated as persons whose lives can be hopeful and whose families can have hope. Here, then, is an institution dedicated to giving patients hope through caring for them as persons.

Caring is a form of love, and to know you are being truly cared for is to know you are being loved. When a person knows he is loved, he has hope. This does not mean that he will expect a cure for his cancer, but he is given courage to feel that life is good and that tomorrow is God's gift of the future. Perhaps through the touch of human care the patient may discover anew the saving love of Christ, the Lord treating him as a precious person. And perhaps his hope will focus beyond this life on unending life with God. Not every taste of hope includes the full menu, but every taste is very important.

Love is also the source of hope in emotional problems. A person burdened with a psychic problem discovers someone who truly cares, and hope begins. Perhaps this is the real secret of how therapy works. No therapist can be sure of being exactly right in a diagnosis: after all, who can really be sure what is happening deep in the heart of another person? But maybe it is not as important as we sometimes think to put a finger on the exact cause of an emotional problem. Maybe what the counselor or friend needs most of all is a plausible diagnosis of the problem and a plausible way to solve it — provided that he really cares for the person and is able to show that he cares. When the patient discovers that his counselor cares, when he feels that his counselor loves, he immediately finds hope for himself. And this may be more important than finding the right label for his problem.

Since loss of hope was probably the deepest cause of the person's difficulty in the first place, the revival of hope brings a revival of the courage needed to face a life in which there is no escape from problems. Love has given the power to hope that life can be worth living in the midst of problems.

Love gives hope to the loving person.

As we have seen, the loving person also needs to hope. So love makes hope both necessary and possible. How does it happen? How does God's love in our lives give us hope today?

In the first place, if we love the world we are compelled to hope for its redemption. The experience of God's love gives us a deep but paradoxical discontent with the way things are. The paradox in love's discontent is that we rejoice in our world *as it is*. We are glad to be in and of this world. We accept it, affirm it, and thank God for it. We love persons around us. But just because we love this distorted and ravaged world, we want better things for it. Thus love's discontent inspires hope for what we love.

We want our neighbors' diseases to be healed, hungry children to have food, captive people to be free. We want refreshment for tired people and salve for the wounds of those who are hurt. We want the wretched of the earth to be made glad. We want the wicked to be saved. Our love for people desires better things for them than their suffering. In this way, love is the beginning of hope. For hope begins with desire, the desire that *wills* others to have what we hope for.

But we have said Christian love must create expectation as well as desire. How does it do this? This is a difficult question, demanding a hard-headed and realistic answer. It is a question intense with urgency, for people often die inside themselves as they lose hope for themselves or others. How can love instil hope for others?

Love sees possibilities that apathy and indifference cannot see. This works on many levels of life. Driven by self-giving love to seek a happier personhood for another, we are able to hear signals in the other person that hint of a will to change. Love keeps us open to possibilities within the loved one. It is only when we lose patience or no longer ever care that we say: "He's hopeless." At another level, when we experience the love of God we feel possibilities for newness on every side. The Spirit of God is the agent of love within us. When God takes us into love's embrace — when all our sins are forgiven, when all our blemished past is accepted, and when we face our future as a tomorrow bathed in the atmosphere of divine love — we are reborn in hope. Desire is transformed into expectancy. We know all things are *possible*. The love the Spirit communicates is the wellspring of hope.

Love is the power that blends desire and expectancy into hope. When love sees possibilities in the loved one, it recognizes these as created by God, whose love is the catalyst that can make all things new (2 Corinthians 5:17). Therefore, as Paul sings, love *hopes* all things.

But we must not slide over the hard cases. Love often gives pain along with hope. This confronts us as one of the stern realities of a loving life. How can love keep a person hoping while a relentless hammering of disappointments beats at his life? This is the cry of loving people in the clutches of personal pain.

A young couple plays with a happy baby. Their eyes are bright with hope for this healthy child; after all, it gets the world's best diet, the world's most expensive medical care, and abundant cultural advantages. They cannot imagine any reason why their dreams should not come true. Several years later, the same couple is bewildered and shocked. The child, now a young adult, has apparently rejected every value the parents hold dear, rejected the style and the ambitions of his parents, indeed rejected the parents themselves. His way of life seems to lead stubbornly toward what his parents feel is self-destruction. The parents are anguished.

The investment of love the parents made in this child was enormous, but in fact their love was in large part self-interested love. They wanted a *return* on their investment, a sense of a parents' job well-done, gratitude, affection, and all the other benefits parents receive from successful children. Now they see no possibilities. All they feel is the cold despair of rejection. They lose hope.

Can love revive hope? Only if it becomes a love that gives without demanding a return on love's investment.

The first test of agapic love is whether it can give the gift of freedom. Love for a daughter must give her freedom to be herself, even with her anger and rebellion against the parents who love her. When love becomes a love that *lets* her be a child in the far country, it becomes a love that might attract her home again. Love gives hope of a homecoming when it lets the other leave home. Love is a power to let selfish hopes die — especially the hopes that are really demands that our dreams come true precisely as we wish them to. Agapic love is the power to revive hope by turning demanding hope into a loving hope.

But there are even stiffer challenges to love's hope-giving power. A father who is ignorant about homosexuality — but knows that he hates and fears it — learns that his adolescent son is homosexual. After lengthy therapy and many prayers, it emerges that his son is a *confirmed* homosexual. The father despairs of any change. Can love for his son keep hope alive?

Two parents weep when they first learn that their little girl is mentally retarded. Years of special education, loving care, and professional counsel leave the daughter a three-year-old child in a twenty-year-old body. Love is real; but how does love keep hope alive?

Love here is the *only* hope. The rebellious daughter gives no hope that she will fulfil any of her parents' dreams for her. Psychiatry gives no hope that the homosexual son can be changed to heterosexual life. Medical science gives no hope that the mentally retarded girl can ever enjoy a well-developed brain. There are no clear *reasons* to hope that what these parents want most will be given them. Hope slips away as the facts become powerful evidence that there should be no hope.

But love hopes all things. The love that lets people be what they are, even when we desperately want them to be different from what they are — *this* love hopes all things. The paradox of love's power is that it sometimes gives new hope only as we let our fondest hopes die.

The parents of the retarded child once desired and expected that something could be done to help their child. Gradually, they lost their expectation, but kept the desire. So strong was this desire that it was really a demand: healing the child was the condition the parents put on God for their own acceptance of him. Now as they experience God's love for themselves they discover that they can give their full, unconditional love to their retarded child. Gradually they let go of their hearts' demand that she be different from what she is. They let the unconditional demand for change melt into unconditional acceptance of what is — the daughter's precious self as *she* is. And now love begins to hope. The script is the same for the parents of the rebellious daughter or the homosexual son.

Love hopes in a new way. This totally accepting love brings hope, not for a miracle of healing, but for the miracle of joy, which is the miracle of gratitude. This love brings hope that life is good, that it has point and meaning, and that the future ahead is one which we can walk into expectantly. In love we learn to *expect* to be surprised by God and joy — along with pain. Love is the power of a new hope that can co-exist with pain.

Love hopes all things. How extravagant is Paul's song! How absurd, in the face of tough realities and expert prognoses, even to speak of such unlimited hope! But love, the power that suffers long without setting limits, is also the power that keeps hoping without setting due dates. Despair comes from deadlines set too early and hope defined too narrowly. Hope fails when love is a demand instead of a gift. Agapic love lets things and people be, and in the gift of letting things and people be love becomes a power that creates a hope that will not disappoint us.

13
Love Endures All Things

LOVE IS THE POWER to endure things we hate. Love does not take hateful things out of our lives; its power works within our lives. If love eliminated everything we hate, we would not need its power to endure them. So again we confront the fact that we experience love *within limits*, the limits set by the realities of our lives. Love is not the secret of escape; it is the power to endure.

The ingredients of endurance are patience and courage.

In biblical experience, enduring has a passive, accepting side called *patience*, and an active, aggressive side called *courage*. In patience we say Yes to life in the midst of evil assaults on our own existence. In courage we counter-attack against the evil that assaults us. To endure is to blend patience and courage in the face of all that hurts us and so to grow into a fuller person.

We are dealing here with more than the mere power to *survive*. Even survival, admittedly, sometimes looks like more than we can manage. But being survivors only means we came through alive, that we managed to hang on, and St. Paul has much more in mind than hanging on. Enduring means growing and expanding as persons under pressure.

Endurance is a very positive accomplishment. Take patience, the passive side of endurance. Patience in the Bible is not a spineless submission to whatever comes along, an inexhaustible willingness to put up with everything. In the face of all that screams out that life is rotten, patience is the power to see some joy, some gladness, some light in the midst of life. It is the power to see point and meaning in living while one's life is under assault.

Patience is completed by courage. Courage is an inner power to resist the painful experiences of life by counter-attacking evil even when we cannot expect to conquer it on our own. Courage keeps us on the offensive while we are forced to be patient.

Without courage patience turns to passivity; without patience courage becomes desperation; enduring takes a prodigious supply of both. This is the picture we get from the Bible. The pious Hebrew seemed to see all of life as waiting time. "I waited patiently for the Lord" (Psalm 40:1); "I wait for the Lord, my soul waits . . ." (Psalm 130:5); "O Lord, be gracious to us; we wait for thee" (Isaiah 33:2). The patient believer waited long and coped with daily disappointment. "We look for light, and behold, darkness" (Isaiah 59:9). Still, the Hebrew heart was a prisoner of hope. Waiting would be rewarded. God would come and prove that he was worth waiting for. "It will be said on that day, 'Lo, this is our God; we have waited for him, that he might save us. This is the Lord; we have waited for him; let us be glad and rejoice in his salvation'" (Isaiah 25:9). "Those who wait for me," the Lord promises, "shall not be put to shame" (Isaiah 49:23).

Hope gives patience its courage. Those who "wait for the Lord shall renew their strength, they shall mount up with wings like eagles" (Isaiah 40:31). When the people were urged to keep waiting, they were always urged on to courage as well. "Wait for the Lord; be strong, and let your heart take courage; yea, wait for the Lord!" (Psalm 27:14).

People in the Christian age need to endure in virtually the same way as the Hebrews did. The bruises of life are still relentless, and the coming of God is deliberate and slow. The author of Hebrews speaks to the condition of many of us when he says: "You endured a hard struggle with sufferings" (Hebrews 10:32). The enduring is, of course, painful. Christ's own passion and cross is a model of Christian endurance (Hebrews 12:2), but his resurrection is a signal of victory through endurance. Salvation lies at the end of the tunnel: The one who endures to the end, said Jesus, will be saved (Matthew 10:22; 24:13).

The Second Letter of Peter tells us about waiting with courage for the coming of the new creation. We wait for God, but God's delay is a delay of love. "Not wishing that any should perish" (3:9), he takes his time. But while we wait for him, as we must, we have to be "hastening the coming of the day of God" (3:12), that is, resisting the forces that resist the power of God's kingdom. "Waiting" and "hastening" are the correlates of patience and courage. And they blend into a strong hope for a new earth where justice finally rules from pole to pole (3:13).

We have come to see the positive power of endurance. The power to endure all things turns out to be the power to live vigorously if not victoriously in the face of evil. It is the power to feel the joy of gratitude in the teeth of violent assault on your happiness. It is the power to move into an energetic counterattack on evil, even though you know that it is too strong for you. It is the power to be hopeful that your life and that of the whole world is headed for redemption. To endure, then, is to live as one who knows that Christ is Lord. This is why the power to endure is the power to love.

Let us look now at the sorts of things love enables us to endure.

Love endures God.

We need, for one thing, to endure God himself. This is a paradox — to say that we have to endure the God who endures us. God works out his purposes in strange ways, slowly, often more silent than communicative. He is invisible, intangible, and inaudible; and his presence often feels like his absence. We have to endure his awful silence and his painful slowness.

Enduring that was often terribly hard for Old Testament people. The golden calf is a gleaming symbol of how difficult it is to endure his invisibility, his intangibility. And the cry of the people echoes through the ages of waiting: "Return, O Lord! How long? Have pity on thy servants!" (Psalm 90:13). If God stays away, how do we know he has not forever left us on our own? "My God, my God, why hast thou forsaken me? Why art thou so far from helping me?" (Psalm 22:1). What is the word of God to such agony? The word is: *Wait!*

To be sure, promises were made, but the promised reality seemed always out of reach. The Lord will save sometime; meanwhile, we can only endure him. They always needed reminding, these Israelites, that God is incomparable, but it was just his incomparable ways that made it so hard to endure him. He was the covenant-partner who would never go back on his covenant, the liberator of the oppressed, the judge who would settle accounts for the poor, the king who would ransom Israel. These were the verbal assurances, but the evidence for them was thin.

Most of us still find it necessary to endure God. Some people see him everywhere: they seem to have a special eye for God's ways and spot him in every corner. They feel that God is poised in the wings of their life's stage, straining to break in whenever he gets their cue. For these people God is not endured, only celebrated. Many people, however, still need to endure God in patience and courage.

Some learn to endure God by working out a rational defense of his strange slowness. We might tell ourselves, for instance, that God will balance suffering with joy in the end. The people who suffer too much now will be rewarded with an overflow of joy in heaven. The measure of joy will compensate for the pain endured below. In this way the harmony of the future helps people to endure God in the present.

But there is a kind of love that will not endure God on the basis of such rational harmony. Out of love for those who suffer much and suffer innocently, some people refuse to endure God's ways now for the sake of harmony later. Atheism can be born of love. Ivan Karamazov in Dostoevsky's great novel was an atheist for the sake of love. The suffering of innocent children was his special horror. "I don't want harmony," he shouted to his brother. "From *love* of humanity, I don't want it. I would rather be left with unavenged suffering." Ivan would rather endure the undeserved suffering of children without God than endure God in the face of it. No harmony that God gave in heaven could pay for the suffering of innocents on earth.

There is deep integrity to such a refusal to endure God. Who has the right answer for Ivan's atheism of love? Alyosha, his believing brother, answers with the only word a Christian finally has to offer. He does not scold Ivan or urge him to be patient or argue on God's behalf. Instead, he loves Ivan and points him to the cross of Christ. He embraces his older brother, and speaks the one word that can be spoken in the silence of God: "But there is a Being and He can forgive everything, all and for all, because He gave His innocent blood for all and everything."

This is the only way to endure the absence and silence of God — the way of faith in God's own suffering. God became incarnate and experienced for himself the need to endure. He, too, had to cry: "My God, my God, why hast thou forsaken me?" In a strange and terrible way God himself suffered the silence and absence of God. He had to endure *with us* his own strange ways. Love was his power to endure all things for us. Only as we become part of his loving can we truly endure him.

Love endures evil.

As love endures God, it also endures the earthly assaults on our lives. We must endure God because he is invisible and intangible. We must endure the assaults on our own lives because they are so painfully visible and tangible. The crisis for us is whether we will endure them in love or merely survive.

We experience assaults on life both privately and globally. Some of them come from nature: we call them natural evils. They may be experienced privately in brain tumors and cancer, globally in world hunger and floods and earthquakes. Other assaults against life come from persons: we call these moral evils, because someone is morally responsible for them. They may be experienced privately in the form of a betrayal by a friend or a painful divorce or direct violence. They may be experienced globally as war, injustice, oppression. In whatever form, we all experience assaults on life.

The ultimate assault on our private lives is death. For some people life on the way to final death is pockmarked by minor deaths. A minor death is the loss of a vital and precious part of one's life. There are many kinds of minor deaths. A man is forced to retire from his life's work when he is still able and eager to do his work creatively. He suffers vocational death. A woman, for whom appearance and sexuality are vital, undergoes a mastectomy. She may suffer a sexual death. A scholar loses his eyesight. He suffers a death of creativity. A couple discovers they cannot have children. They suffer genetic death. None of us escapes minor deaths. The path to life's end is strewn with minor deaths.

Physically we manage to survive our minor deaths, but *enduring* takes unusual inner power. To achieve endurance — through patience and courage — requires the power of love.

Let us first mention some things love does not do for us in the face of our minor deaths. Love does not give us instant reasons for going on. A woman does not drive home from her husband's funeral with her head clear about the logic of the goodness of life. Love certainly has nothing to do with quick calculations to add up more blessings than curses. Rather, love is the power — gradually and in complete honesty about how rotten life can be — to discover that life has point, has joy, has hope, has deep, untapped promises of goodness; and that therefore we can sing a doxology to God.

Love is not a magic power that turns bad things into good things. Love does not send us on a hallucinogenic trip that makes horrid things look beautiful. God's love is honest love.

The evil we endure in the power of love *is* evil. We only subvert the love force if we try to use it to twist evil things into tolerably good things.

The first act of love's courage in confrontation with evil is the honesty, in God's own presence, to look evil in the face and call it evil. How do we dare call evil what our piety tells us God has laid on us as a cross to bear? We dare because we know in the depths of our heart that evil, whether natural or personal, is always evil. Love gives us power to say No to any nonsense about the ultimate goodness of evil, because it knows that God's will is opposed to all that brings unjust and needless harm to his children. So love's courage to endure begins with the courage to see evil as the evil it is.

Second, courage is the power of love in active resistance to evil. Of course, courage cannot change the sheer fact of evil; it cannot restore sight or replace an amputated leg or bring back a dead husband. But courage *is* the power to defeat the second evil that the first evil always tries to create. The evil of a child's death threatens to create in parents the evil of believing that there will never again be reason to smile. The evil of blindness creates the second evil of the scholar's despair of creative living. The evil of a mastectomy creates the second evil of a fear of sexual loss. Courage resists these evils that evil creates. Assaults on life can have a chain reaction, and courage breaks the chain.

Third, courage is love's power to re-create reality. Courage is the power of a blind person to seize the world around and see it in ways that the retina of the human eye can never discover. Courage is the power of a childless couple to see their present lives as so significant that they do not need heirs with their name to give them a future. Courage is the power to see oneself and one's spouse as captives of a love that does not rely on a perfect human body. Courage is the power to grasp the intense beauty and goodness of family, friends, animals, and plants, even when we are told that a newly discovered cancer will cut us off from all of these in a few months. Personal courage re-creates reality because it learns to see reality in ways reborn in love.

We have just been talking of private evils, but love must endure global evils, too. In fact, only love has to endure them, for only love feels their pain. The way to escape the challenge of enduring global evil is to tune out love. Only love feels the agony of a famine in China or tidal wave in India.

Courage is love's power to resist the evils that help bring about global pain: the selfish waste of food and energy by some while others are trapped by famine and underdevelopment, oppressive political power, economic systems that strangle poor people with hopelessness. Courage resists global evil by resisting the realities that cause or contribute to it. Enduring all things requires us to join the struggle against the powers that threaten other people's endurance.

Courage needs patience, however, just as patience needs courage. When we confront global evil we know that our own courage cannot fundamentally cure the world's deep disharmony. This is neither cynicism nor defeatism, but realism about ourselves. But love also hopes that God does intend to heal the global disease and to reconcile *all* things to himself (Colossians 1:20). It is a form of waiting on the Lord.

This is why Christian endurance of evil must be a blend of patience with courage. Courage alone would waste its power by settling only for total victory now; patience alone would eventually accept evil as our inescapable destiny. Together they are the power to accept life in the face of evil and to fight the evil that threatens life. Patience makes courage realistic; courage gives patience a sting.

Enduring evil is not at all like wanting evil. As we noted earlier, we sometimes want the evil of suffering. We all feel a neurotic desire to suffer sometimes, for suffering rewards us with such sweet pity, such flattering attention from our friends. But love is not the power to accept the rewards of suffering. It is the power to endure what we hate.

Our model is Jesus. He endured all things in the power of love. We can see in him what happens when love endures evil. Love drove him toward others without demand for return on his investment. He came with clear-eyed desire to be a servant (Philippians 2:5-7), came into a world of suffering as a genuine human participant. Coming in love for others, he was bound to be touched at least, perhaps consumed by the evil that consumed them.

Jesus endured suffering. He did not wish to suffer, nor did he call attention to his suffering in order to enjoy the world's pity. Jesus was not a masochist nor a parasite on the pity of friends. He prayed for escape from the cross, and when he suffered he asked for no tears. At the foot of Calvary, with pious women crying for him, he looked at them and said: "Do not weep for me, but weep for yourselves" (Luke 23:28).

Agapic love always leads us into suffering. To choose love is in a sense to choose suffering, even though it never means to want suffering. Love drives us toward the suffering of others without demands for reward. This makes us vulnerable, as Christ was vulnerable. Moved by love, we are bound to suffer with and suffer for others; and when that happens we suffer with Christ — the form of suffering that qualifies us for a share in Christ's kingdom (Romans 8:17). Suffering with Christ in the power of his love, we have the power to endure the things we hate — just as he endured them.

Love endures God's delays. Love endures the "slings and arrows of outrageous fortune" directed against us privately. Love endures global evils. Love endures the suffering that comes to us in sharing the suffering of others. Love endures because love is the power of the life of the suffering Christ. "It is no longer I who live, but Christ who lives in me" (Galatians 2:20). *Christ in us* is the secret of the love that endures all things.

14
Love Lasts

LOVE ABIDES. It never fails. Love is the one power in this life that is self-generating. It is the one reality in time that goes into eternity unchanged. Love will never need to be transformed into something better. Because love is the one perfect eternal reality, it abides throughout this life and into the next in its simple form — the power that moves us toward another without expecting a reward.

Agapic love cannot die because it is divine.

Loving without reward is not a power that comes to human beings naturally: by nature we move toward people to satisfy our own deepest needs. We need to be loved, to be wanted, to be cared for, and we move toward those who give us signals that they can provide us such attention. Needing to be completed, we seek to become with someone else what we cannot be alone. We need to grow toward a higher human level of experience, so we reach beyond what we have been to what we still can be. And we move to those whose love will help us reach. This is erotic love. But the power to move toward another only for his or her sake is the power of God's agapic love. It *is* God himself working in us, so it is perfection.

It cannot die; nor can it be improved. It is the self-energizing heart of the universe.

If we are nudged by love to seek the good of another purely for that person's sake, we have been moved by God. If we have even a fleeting impulse to forget our self-interest and act solely for another, with no regard for any reward, we are in touch with the core of cosmic reality. If we are driven by a desire to heal or help another, and are glad when that person is helped even if no one knows or cares that it was we who helped, we are under the influence of almighty God. If we can keep caring for the person even if he forgets completely that he owes us anything at all, we have been sustained by God. We are being seized by the one power that never runs down, wears out, or requires supplemental energy; it is the energy that catalyzes all other sources of energy. Hence, love cannot die.

Erotic love dies because it is human.

Human love, of course, does die. Eros flickers and fades as the winds of desire rise and wane. Change is the way of life for eros. This indeed is part of the power of eros. Its very fragility creates the possibility of repeated excitement. We could not endure a steady stream of eros at its highest pitch: we need the valleys to be inspired by the peaks.

If eros keeps waning it will eventually die. When the loved one no longer wills to meet the lover's needs, eros dies slowly. When the loved one leaves and does not come back, eros dies for lack of stimulation. When the lover has no more need of what the loved one wills to give, eros dies. Nourished by needs within the lover and the promise offered by the loved one, erotic love has no self-generating power. It is powerful, but it is not a power in itself.

We need not think less of erotic love just because it is mortal. Erotic love, in all its forms, is the driving power for personal growth. It may not endure unchanged into eternity, but its unrelenting urges move us beyond ourselves in this life. All creativity rises from the need-power of eros. Eros is a drive created by human need for a share in what is beautiful; it is life's aesthetic power. Eros is a drive formed by human need for truth; it is life's scientific power. Eros is a drive rising from human need for personal completion and human communion — through sex, friendship, or family. But eros dies precisely because it is a power born of need. When need is satisfied, eros dies.

This never happens completely on earth. It happens only in snippets and only while we are strong. Eros relaxes only for a brief moment, and even then only fragments of our needs are wholly met. An artist may sometimes be fleetingly satisfied at some aspect of his work, but he is soon driven by a creative need to seek other visions. Sexual eros is sated for a moment, but is soon revived; and even in the moment of its orgasmic satisfaction huge spiritual areas of one's life can be gasping for something more. Eros never dies on earth by being permanently satisfied. It dies only of neglect or abuse. It dies when the vigors of the human body and spirit atrophy in old age or illness. It dies in those people who have been deceived by the demon that confuses physical lust with human eros.

All gifts but love are relative.

In his love song Paul holds love up against the background of three other gifts from God. He does not disparage these others: prophecy, tongues, and knowledge are good and useful gifts within the Christian community, for which God should be thanked. Paul's point is that they are *relative*. They are not the one thing needful.

Paul thought that the Corinthian Christians set too high a premium on prophesying, speaking in strange tongues, and knowing the secrets of God. People who had the gift for these things were considered very significant in the church there. Anybody could love, they figured; only special people spoke in tongues or knew the secrets of God. Paul knew better. An "ordinary" person, set in motion only by another person's need, is in a class with God. The gifts that put a person on stage are second-class. This gift is always absolute; the others will someday be obsolete.

Paul does not say that prophecies, tongues, and knowledge will be destroyed in the coming of the kingdom. That fate is reserved for evil: the coming of God never causes a loss of something good. But some good things are imperfect, and when the perfect comes it will transform all imperfection. Prophecy, tongues, and human knowledge — good gifts, all — are imperfect. Hence, while they will not be destroyed as if they were evil, they will need radical transformation.

Take prophecy, for example. Some people are apparently given special insight into the ways of God and the meaning of events. They are moved to interpret what God is doing in the world and what he wants done by human beings. When they speak, they have authority. Ordinary folk recognize the gift of prophecy and respect it. Now although there is no checklist to enable you to identify a real prophet beyond doubt, people within the circle of faith could discern when the gift was real, else the prophetic voice would have fallen flat. The community, alive to the Spirit, was expected to tell the difference between an inspired prophet and a self-inflated guru.

In any case, Paul was not about to deflate prophecy. He himself was sometimes seized by the Spirit's inspiration, so he could not simply dismiss others who claimed to be prophets and whom the people believed. Besides, the very phenomenon is a wonder. Nobody knows what happens when a person is inspired. Nobody can explain how one person gains unique insights into the deeper meaning of things and how these insights are recognized by others as revelation. This is a mystery about any person who has unique discernment. But in prophecy we see the further wonder of God's allowing real people to see with his eyes and then to speak his word through their human voices.

Prophecy may be a splendid gift, but it is not the ideal way of discerning and communicating God's will. In a perfect world, every person would be attuned to God. Every nudge of conscience would relay his will; every insight would be divine illumination. We would need no special prophets. Thus, when the "perfect" is come, says Paul, prophecy will have had its day. The lights are turned off when the sun rises.

Speaking in tongues was never high on Paul's list of Christian needs, but he knew that for some people it was a liberating spiritual experience which enabled them to reach beyond the ordinary boundaries of their consciousness. The speaker in tongues makes sounds that to a casual listener may seem like gibberish, but what these sounds seem to a reason-bound person to be does not matter. What matters is that the sounds are signals of a deep spiritual experience beyond reason. The "tongues" are part of one's freedom from ordinary, brain-controlled self-expression.

But love is in another class. Ecstasy is private pleasure, enjoyed by a few now and then; love is universal service, open to everyone all the time. Ecstasy thrusts me outside my ordinary world; love drives me into the ordinary world. Ecstasy will fade away as love moves from strength to strength. The one way for ecstasy to survive is to get into love's orbit. And this, of course, is ecstasy's Christian possibility. Ecstasy can become the servant of love, and it does when it liberates someone from the prison cell of ego needs so that he or she can relish the freedom of love's concern for the needs of other people.

The gift of knowledge, too, is a tentative thing. This is Paul's most radical break with the conventional wisdom of his Greek contemporaries. For if any shade of eternity were present here, they thought, it had to be knowledge, particularly knowledge about eternal truth. Now Paul comes to say that our knowledge of God is temporal, limited, and imperfect. What we know of God now is never quite in focus; the details are unclear; the image is shaky. We see through a glass darkly, and we know in fragments — bits and pieces of theology strung together by logic.

We do know some things, of course. Paul himself proclaimed the gospel of God's grace as something he really knew. We know enough to tell people — and remind ourselves — that God wills their salvation. But much of what we know besides this is tentative, correctable, open to change; and it will need radical transformation once we see the truth whole and clear.

But the point of all this talk of knowing and tongue-speaking and prophecy is that love alone is the true standard for Christian experience. We have to let this sink into our souls. For if we are honest we will admit that we prize talents which set us on stage for public praise more than we want to love.

Everything we do and say in our religious life is child's play and prattle by comparison with the final reality ("when the perfect comes"). We are all children. Charismatics clap their hands, make strange sounds, and are tenderly seized by the Spirit of God — in unquestionably real experience. Theologians stammer about God like an adolescent pontificating about ultimate reality — and say unquestionably significant things. Moralists tell people precisely what they ought to do as confidently as a small girl playing mother to her dolls — and give unquestionably good counsel. But then all of them are tempted to spoil their gift by claiming that it is the only reality, the only truth, and the only really necessary gift. We cannot bring ourselves to believe Paul when he tells us that our most serious Christian claims are "childish" play, and that one day we will recognize that they are.

Only love is the sure sign of maturity in Christ. Any person who feels a pull toward another, an urge to care simply because the other is there, is in touch with eternity. The wife who cannot stop caring for a husband, even after he has long bruised her life and ignored her needs, after eros is dead, is in tune with the essence of God. The parent whose heart expands in loving affirmation of a rebellious child, grown now into an estranged adult who gives no affection in return, is sharing divine perfection. The business person who is able to see through the conflicts of competition to a hurting soul within a competitor is living on the fringes of heaven.

This is why love will abide, eternally the same, when all the values we prize have died or been lifted into new stages of perfection. When will our eyes be opened, our minds released, to see love as God's essence and life's perfection? When will we really know? We will not come to this truth by argument, by reasoning from true premises to correct conclusions. We will come to see the truth of love when we are seized by the act of love. When we are in fact loved by the love made visible at the cross of Christ, when we accept this love, we will know that here is the perfect thing which has come to us.

We cannot live by love alone. The power of love does not drive all other legitimate inclinations out of our lives. Nor do we have to be perfect in love to be in perfect love. To experience agapic power at all is to experience the greatest thing in the world; it is to be one with God — for that loving moment. Later, one day, we will love perfectly with perfect love. For now, it is enough that perfect love is here.

15
Program Notes

AS I TRIED to trace how the lyrical ideal of love can work within the limits of life's realities, I was guided by a few fundamental features of divine love. With these in mind, we can bridge the gap between love's unreachable perfection and the valid human realities within which it must do its agapic work. I have waited until now to set these forth explicitly, rather than doing that at the beginning. I wanted readers to move into the substance of the love song without theoretical preliminaries. I add them now in the form of program notes to God's love song. They will, I hope, set in a final sharp focus what I mean when I call this book *Love Within Limits*.

Agapic love is selfless love.

Agapic love is the love modeled by God in his gracious self-giving. We have used a simple definition of this love: *the power that moves us to respond to a neighbor's needs with no expectation of reward*. Giving of itself, it asks no return on its investment. It ignores the subtle calculations of human love; it is not interested in the odds of getting some self-satisfaction in return for its efforts. It gives, not in the hope of inspiring the loved one to give in turn, but simply because the other is there and in need.

The jargon of agape can be so soothing that its absolute demands float through our minds like a misty ideal that never quite settles into a specific possibility. In fact we do not take easily to agape. Laid on us as a demand, it is a formidable weight; promised as a possibility, it may not even be attractive. Consider well: we are called to a love that will move us to move toward others with no expectation of any reward. At the risk of caricature, let us draw a simple example in order to be sure of what this love might ask of us.

Any mother's love for her children is crisscrossed with varied motives that run back and forth between her conscious intentions and subconscious needs. Only God could sort out all the motivations within it. We might agree that normal mother-love has at least a strain of agape in it, but can she love with no expectation of reward? Does agape drive even mothers beyond the borders of human potential?

Here is a modern mother who surely loves her children. She sacrifices all sorts of things for them. She gives up the fashionable clothes her fine tastes covet, the evenings of entertainment she used to enjoy. She forgoes expensive decorations in her house. More important than these, she sacrifices a career for herself. And what does all this go for? Piano lessons and summer camp and braces to straighten crooked teeth and tuition at a fine college. She gives herself, in short, so that her children will look good and do well according to the values of their world. Far more important, she gives *herself*, in care, concern, and endless affection. Surely her love is a giving love.

But she also expects something from her love's investment. Perhaps her love is so refined that all she wants is for her children to make creative use of the gifts they were given. But does not her love allow her to look forward to enjoying their successes? May she not expect them to have, on looking back, some respect and appreciation for her sacrifices? Does she not have the right to expect some affection, happy visits after they are on their own, some telephone calls, a share in the affection of her grandchildren? Does agape forbid us even such small expectations of rewards from a career of self-giving?

No one followed the line of agape to its logical ends with more rigor than Søren Kierkegaard, from whose classic *The Works of Love* I adapted the example of mother-love. Kierkegaard said that living in agape is like paying off an infinite debt. An infinite debt, of course, can never be paid off by a finite person; indeed, since infinity never gets smaller, it cannot even be reduced. Hence, we love without looking forward to a time when the debt is paid off and we can begin looking for credit of our own. Love gives, knowing that it will *never* come to a time when it can finally ask something for itself. This is the unique character of agapic love: it gives without demand of *any* return. We must see agape in this pure form, or we will dissolve it into need-love and eventually lose it altogether.

All other loves are different from agape in one crucial way: they all arise from a need and a desire for love's reward. This single ingredient unites all human loves as variations of the one natural love we have been calling eros. Eros is a ladder we climb to reach heights beyond our incomplete selves. Eros reaches out to another because the other promises to fill a need. The power of eros is an energy bred of anxiety. The power of human love is the power that moves us to unite with someone else, or something else, in order to let the other fill an emptiness in our being.

Romantic love, of course, is eros. Emerging from some biological source that we loosely label libido, it moves upward in desire for union with another person. No love more consciously seeks reward. Romantic love involves self-giving, but only with a promise that the loved one will give in kind.

Friendship, too, is eros. At its best the love of friends is formed by a mutual trust and fidelity so unique in human relations that we often suppose it to be essentially different from eros. But friendship, too, is born of need, and in this respect at least is a form of eros. All of us need a friend, someone who will be there with us and for us, who will trust and care for us. We need someone to share privacy and intimacy, someone who will always be on our side. We give

ourselves to a friend, it is true; but in giving we expect friendship to be given in turn.

Family love is eros. No father or mother ever wanted a
child purely for the child's sake. No child ever loved a parent
outside the context of its need for security, of touch, of food,
and of affection. Self-giving also permeates family love; God
himself took the title Father to signal his self-giving care for
his children. But found on earth, family love is need-love.
Even this love is fed by expectation of love given in return.

Love for God is eros. We love God because he alone promises to fill our soul's potential. Earlier we quoted Augustine's
famous phrase about the restless heart, which pushes us
Godward in expectation of rest at last. We are all God-seekers
because we need to be fulfilled by him. We may not know
where to find him. Some of us settle with poor substitutes for
him. But our need drives us relentlessly to seek him, and we
expect eternal happiness when we find him.

Eros is a good love, not an evil one. It is a gift of God built
into our creaturely incompleteness, driving us to seek what is
good and true and beautiful, and to create communion with
others. It stretches us beyond the confines of our own egos. To
be sure, it is restless, anxious, and turbulent. It can be reduced
to lust and distorted into the use of someone else as a tool
instead of an affirmation of him as a sovereign individual free
to withhold from us as well as give to us. Eros can be bent and
broken, and in our sinful world it almost always is. But eros
is good. It is the creative power in all that lives and grows,
all that brings color, vigor, and explosive joy to human life.
I mean here to reject the extreme Protestantism that praises
agape in order to make eros look ungodly. I want to stress that
when God's love song celebrates agape, it does not mean us
to despise eros; to praise divine love is not to condemn human
love.

The love of God's love song, however, is the love that gives
without expectation of return. This is what sets it off from all
other loves. But who is competent for such love? If this is the
ideal, and if it is truly expected of us regularly and consis-

tently, we are lost. So we must observe some other basic facts about this love.

The love of our song is power.

Love is a power that flows into persons and drives them to move toward others. Love enables people to do loving sorts of things and be loving sorts of persons. That love is a power explains why Paul personifies it, talking as if love itself did things. Love believes, he says. And love endures, hopes, and bears all things. What he obviously means is that love is the power which enables people to endure, to believe, and to hope. Knowing that love is a power can reduce the burden of love as a duty. The song does not crystallize the perfections of love into a profile of a perfectly loving person and then pin us down with a duty to be that sort of person now, regularly and predictably.

This is not to ignore the Christian *obligation* of love. Jesus called his disciples into the life of self-denying love when he said: "A new commandment I give to you, that you love one another; even as I have loved you" (John 13:34). And this is only one of many declarations of the law of love. No question about it: love is a duty as well as a power. But the good news is that love is power. Love *enables* us to do what love obligates us to do.

We should not view love as power as though it were some sort of psychic current surging from its own generators through the network of the universe. Love does not exist on its own; there is no love "out there" by itself. It is not a drive or instinct pushing its way into our lives from some benign abyss within our subconscious. Nor, we must add, is it a primeval myth. Agapic love is not a metaphor expressing our primitive wish for a kinder world. This love is a personal ingredient central to the being of almighty God. Love is a power because *God* is love.

Agapic love, therefore, is the central, dominant, and ulti-mately irresistible power of the universe. Love is more powerful than evil. Love is more basic than the need for fairness and the demand for equity: love always drives us toward justice, but justice does not drive us to love. Agape is the power within God that maintains the ultimacy of his free benevolence. It is the power in God that enables him freely to move toward inferior creatures who have made themselves sinners, and to move toward them for their good, with no demand for a return on his investment. The promise of power implied in 1 Corinthians 13, then, is the promise of the ultimate and unconquerable force of the universe.

The love of our song is God's love.

St. Paul did not write this love song after sustained and sensitive observation of how love works in human society. His portrait is not drawn from sketches he made of people around him. His model was God in loving action toward us.

This makes it very clear that the love of God's love song needs to be *believed*. The promise of love's power is received only in an astounding act of faith. There is no sure evidence in the media's account of world affairs that agapic love is stronger than evil. General Motors has not leaked the secret that agapic love is the key to its corporate greatness. We have not discovered personally — through introspection or through psychoanalysis — that agapic love is dominant in our lives over all other drives and desires. Love as ultimate power is an article of faith — and it takes a lot of believing. There is only one thing that can give us faith like this; it is love itself. The power to believe in love is love. But at this point, the power of love is love received. It works in us, not as our power to act in love, but as our willingness to be loved.

This brings us down to evangelical fundamentals: faith in love comes only after a soul's journey to Christ's cross, where God's love breaks through for what it is. Agape is central to God's very being and is the ultimate expression of his character. But our praise of agape should not blind us to God's erotic love. God loves erotically in the finest sense of that word. He

loved his only Son with a love that brought him great pleasure: "Thou art my beloved Son; with thee I am well pleased"
(Mark 1:11). He loved his creation with divine zest: again and
again Genesis repeats that God saw that the created world was
good. We do not know what it is like to be God. And we do not
know the precise psychic dynamics in God's heart and mind
when he loves. We may be sure that God loves erotically
without the desperate needs of human eros. But we may
suppose that he loves with genuine desire for his loved ones
and the pleasure they give him in fellowship and praise.

On the other hand, it would be false to picture God as
loving on two separate tracks. God has only one love, for he is
the ultimately integrated and whole self. But his love for us
has to take on the nature of a sacrificial love because in our sin
we lost our original attractiveness. This love is God's power to
transcend the needs of eros. It is God's self, moving outward
by the power of his own being, to seek the salvation of his
sinful creatures without demand for the pleasure of a great
return on his sacrifice.

Agapic love works within the limits of human life.

We do not and cannot live by agapic love alone. Nor can we
manage a total surrender to the power of agape. We cannot, in
this life, be all that agape has the power to make us. The ideal
of the agapic person never becomes the real you or the real me.
There are two reasons why agape, even when it becomes the
dominant power in our lives, cannot be the only one.

The first reason is our human weakness, which is a combination of our finitude and our sinfulness. We are not God; we
are severely limited creatures trying to manage our lives
within the limits set for us by our inherited personalities and
our social situations. But not only are we limited creatures, we
are sinful as well. Our sin debilitates our will to love. It is
centered resolutely in a stubborn pride that does not like to
surrender to a selfless love. Love must do its work within

the limits created by our human weaknesses. The upshot is that we cannot realistically expect to be the ideal lover profiled in St. Paul's hymn of love.

The second reason we cannot live totally and only by agapic love is that we must live by powers and demands alongside of and different from agape. Two of these cropped up repeatedly in our excursion through the lyrics of agape: erotic love and justice. We have an irresistible, compelling need to become more than we are, and to achieve that growth through union with another person, or with God, or with something in between. This is eros. We cannot do without it, nor does agapic love move us to try. Agapic love must do its work within the limits created by eros.

Moreover, we have a primeval demand for fairness. This desire is not as turbulent as the need for personal union, but now and then it does rise to an agonized crescendo. At some moment of pained awareness of man's inhumanity to man each of us utters the scream of the soul that life is grotesquely unfair. Invaded by agape, a person will recoil at injustice done to other people. But even when the cry for justice includes a plea for one's own rights, agapic love does not muffle the sound. Love is limited by justice.

Agapic love does not preempt the space in our lives taken by erotic love and justice. Love works *within the limits* of natural life, and this is why we cannot live by sacrificial love alone.

Agape slips into life through crevices in our egos — those chinks left open between the solid blocks of self-interest. It filters through a grid of our weakness, our needs, and our claims on life. Agape respects all these realities, does its work within them. Love does not destroy nature; it transforms it.

Once inside our reality, however, love changes everything. It does not change by negation, but by adding a transforming dimension. To erotic love it adds an unselfish desire for the good of the loved one even while it leaves us free to seek our needs. It makes eros even more restless, but with a restlessness born not only of our unfulfilled needs but also of our loved one's unfulfilled needs. Agape also leaves us discontented with mere justice. For it moves us toward personal closeness with those who suffer injustice, and through this closeness opens our hearts more acutely to their total needs.

When agape does its work, our erotic drive toward attractive people will be tempered by a will for the welfare of people who are not attractive. Our strident claims on life will be muted by a sensitive giving to life. Our demands for what we have coming to us will be blended with a desire equally strong that others get what they have coming to them.

Our experience of agapic power will be in fits and starts. Our achievements will be in fragments. The impulse of agape will move in and out of our more self-centered impulses, restraining them, correcting them, redirecting them, but not killing them. For a moment here and a moment there we will sense that we are being driven by the love that expects no reward; then other motives will intrude, other needs will press us, and other rightful demands will complicate our love. We are not likely to manage long days of uncompromised agape. Our lives will not likely be so consistently dominated by agape that we can be predictable and consistent lovers in the divine style of sacrificial love. But love is a power that keeps moving us in that direction.

Let me repeat this: love is a *power* that moves *within* the limits set by our human weakness and human power. Nothing is more important than that we understand and accept this truth about love. If we perceive Christian love only as lofty obligation we will be crushed by it, for agape by itself is an impossible ideal. We never manage life exclusively by self-giving love.

To be condemned by love is a terrible irony, for love is the very power of acceptance. But we are condemned by love when it comes to us only in the form of a law, because it is the most utterly impossible of all laws. None of us can make it as persons who care for others with utter disregard for any reward for ourselves. The only way to cope with love as a law is to experience it first as a gift.

Sinners can live before the face of ideal love only by living in the power of love itself. For love is the power to live gladly as imperfect lovers. Not only is love the power to forget oneself in concern for others, it is also the power to forgive oneself for not forgetting oneself. This power is the love of God for us in the form of crucified love, the love we discover when we see Christ's cross as God's entrance into our lives with a love that forgives *all*. When we have the power to accept this love, we have the power to accept ourselves gladly as weak persons who cannot easily manage to love as God loves us.

In the courage born of accepting love, we can look love's ideal full in the face, admit we do not measure up to it, and yet yield ourselves again and again to love as the power that pushes us very gradually toward it. With this courage, we can cope with the unending job of finding our way through the complex network of our duties, demands, and drives, through life's crisscrossing desires and needs, toward a life increasingly disposed to love others without demanding a return on our investment.